Challenge

The following Jesuits contributed to CHALLENGE:
John R. Crocker, Thomas J. Diehl,
Howard J. Gray, Robert F. Gross,
Robert J. Lab, Mark J. Link, John A. Lucal,
Christopher F. Mooney,
James A. O'Brien, James K. Serrick, Thomas F. Shea,
Thomas J. Sweeney, and Joseph A. Tetlow.

Without Martin I. Carrabine, S.J., who guided us
through the planning, writing, and
publishing of CHALLENGE, *the book would not*
now be published.

CHALLENGE

JOHN W. O'MALLEY, S.J.
EDWARD J. MC MAHON, S.J.
ROBERT E. CAHILL, S.J.
CARL J. ARMBRUSTER, S.J.

Loyola University Press

Chicago, Illinois

Imprimi Potest
WILLIAM J. SCHMIDT, S.J.
Provincial of the Chicago Province
November 8, 1957

Nihil Obstat
AUSTIN G. SCHMIDT, S.J.
Censor Deputatus
November 11, 1957

Imprimatur
✠ SAMUEL CARDINAL STRITCH
Archbishop of Chicago
November 12, 1957

Challenge

A PRAYER BOOK

This book is meant to help you respond to the challenge of Christ and to help you to a prayerful apostolate. CHALLENGE is a prayer book which aims at more than the mere reading and rote recitation of prayers. By setting some of the finest prayers of all Christendom into context and by inviting you to use them as material for reflection and meditation, as well as for recitation, CHALLENGE hopes to help you make these prayers your own. You thus begin to share the beautiful aspirations of the great friends of God and take the first step toward flooding your whole life with a spirit of prayer. A printed prayer is only a half prayer; to be a whole prayer it must be felt and lived.

Many prayers in CHALLENGE are taken from *The Raccolta*. These prayers are identified by the reference printed at the end of each: [R. 258]. The number 258 shows where the prayer is printed in *The Raccolta*. The indulgence, if the prayer carries one, is also indicated within the brackets. Prayers from sources other than *The Raccolta* are credited to their authors. No individual acknowledgment is made for prayers written by the authors of CHALLENGE.

TABLE

OF CONTENTS

The present time demands Catholics without fear,
to whom it is a thing supremely
natural to confess their faith openly
in word and in deed every time the law
of God and regard for Christian honor demand it.
Real men, whole men, strong and fearless!
Not men who are men by halves . . .
Pope Pius XII

The Challenge

This is My challenge!
This is My challenge to the Catholic men and
    women of today
as expressed by My vicar on earth.
This is My challenge
which dares you to be rid of half measures,
which dares you to strive for the fullness of
    Christian perfection.

"The present time demands Catholics
    without fear . . ."
"The present time demands . . . Real men,
    whole men, strong and fearless!"
My vicar calls for Catholic men and women
who draw their strength from prayer and
    the sacraments,
who draw their strength from a close union with Me.
The true and perfect Christian combines
    prayer and apostolate.
The true and perfect Christian is
prayerful in his apostolate and
    apostolic in his prayer,

for he hopes to channel to others
faith and divine life—things divine.
The true and perfect Christian heeds My warning
of the Last Supper
that without Me he can do nothing.

Today's turmoil, says My vicar, demands
Catholics of action, Catholics of prayer.
Today's turmoil demands Catholics of
prayerful action.
That is My challenge to you!

THE PLAN

OF THE BOOK

Today Jesus Christ challenges me to be a whole man, a man prayerful in action. He prepares me to respond to His challenge by His gifts, especially sanctifying grace and numerous actual graces.

God has shown, continues to show His infinite love for me. He created me, Christ redeemed me. Our Lord instituted His Church to safeguard me, His sacraments to give me grace.

Through grace God comes to me: God the Father, God the Son, God the Holy Spirit. *Father* "But if one of you asks his father for a loaf, will he hand him a stone?" (Luke 11:11). *Son* "Behold this Heart which has so loved men. If only they would make Me some return for My love . . ." *Holy Spirit* "But the Advocate, the Holy Spirit, whom the Father will send in my name, he will teach you all things, . . ." (John 14:26).

Jesus Christ gave me His Mother as my mother. Mary always understands me, always teaches me to imitate and to love her divine Son.

God gives me countless examples to prove His challenge can be met: those who now enjoy heaven yet wish, through me, to work for God's kingdom— the Saints Triumphant. Those who now suffer in purgatory and need my prayers as I need theirs—the Saints Suffering. Those still living in this world who depend on my prayers as I on their prayers—the "Saints" Militant.

Our Lord gives me the means to preserve, to increase, and to spread His gifts. I guard these gifts by my examen, a plan to discover my weakness and to strengthen my life of grace. I go to confession, the sacrament that washes my soul of sin, increases in me God's grace. I attend Mass—the increase of the Christ-life in which I offer myself with Christ, and then receive Him into my very soul and body. In my prayer I come to know our Lord better, to love Him more ardently, to follow Him more closely. By my apostolate I spread God's gifts. I think as Christ thought; I become zealous for the salvation of all men, working for them, praying for them.

Soon I begin to recognize all that God has given me, is giving me. I faintly understand the gift of the Christ-life God's love gives me. Gladly I now strive to preserve, to increase this Christ-life. Dedicated as I am to a life of service to my King, under the patronage of His Queen, I look with great confidence to the future.

Creation and Grace

In the beginning was the Word,
and the Word was with God;
and the Word was God.
He was in the beginning with God.
All things were made through Him;
without Him was made nothing that was made.

I am the Word of God,
the Second Person of the Blessed Trinity.
I am the only-begotten Son of God,
born of the Father before all ages,
God of God,
Light of light,
true God of true God,
of one being with the Father
by whom all things were made.
I am the alpha and the omega,
the beginning and the end.
I have existed in a union of love
with My Father and the Holy Spirit
from all eternity.

And We willed to share Our love;
We willed to share Our happiness and Our life.
We created others with whom to share them.

1

First We created the choirs of angels:
seraphim, cherubim, and thrones,
to unite themselves to Us in praise and adoration;
dominations, virtues, and powers,
to mirror Our own infinite perfections;
principalities, archangels, and angels,
to care for the other creatures We would fashion.

Then We created man
in Our own image and likeness.
We formed man of the slime of the earth
and breathed into his face the breath of life;
and man became alive.
We planted a paradise of happiness,
a paradise for man whom We had formed.

And We blessed man and said to him:
Increase and multiply,
and fill the earth and subdue it,
and rule the fishes of the sea, the birds of the air,
and all living creatures that move upon the earth.
And We saw all the things that We had made,
We saw that they were very good.

But man rebelled.
He raised his hand to strike at Me, his God.
Man repaid Me evil for My good,
and hatred for My love.
Man sinned,
and now he had to pay the price of sin:
cursed was the earth;
by the sweat of his brow man must earn bread;
man must taste death,
and, being dust, into dust he must return.
Man lost My grace,
and was sad upon the earth.

I loved man
with an everlasting love.
I wanted to turn his mourning into joy,
to console him and make him joyful after his sorrow.
I wanted to reopen the gates of heaven
and return to man the gift of My grace,
so man could again love Me perfectly in return.

My Father so loved man
as to send Me,
His only-begotten Son,
that whoever believed in Me would not perish
but would have everlasting life.
And so, in the fullness of time,
I, the Word of God,
the desired of all the nations,
took upon Myself human flesh
and was born in Bethlehem of the Virgin Mary.
I was called Jesus,
and I would save My people from their sins.

I lived a life of toil, poverty, and sorrow,
but also a life of happiness and love
for I delighted to be with the sons of men.

I came to seek and to save that which was lost
and to give Myself as a ransom.
As the good shepherd
I came to lay down My life for My sheep.
Greater love than this no one has,
that one lay down his life for his friends.
I died for all;
I gave Myself a redemption for all
to make peace through the blood of My cross
and win back a share of the divine life of grace
—for man.

Millions of men shared in that first insult to
    My goodness,
but millions share My redemptive act of love
    on the cross,
so that, if they wish,
they can again share My divine life,
the life of grace.

Among these millions there is
you,
whom I love with an everlasting love;
you,
for whom alone
I would have become man and died on the cross;
you,
not redeemed with gold and silver,
but with My precious blood,
as of a lamb unspotted and undefiled;
you,
the sinner,
whose heart will never rest
until it rests in Me;
you,
for whom I came
that you might have life,
and have it more abundantly.

For you I instituted My Church
to spread the life of grace through the sacraments.
I gave My Church power:
in baptism to remove original sin,
that grace enter your purified soul;
in confirmation to strengthen the life of grace,
that you become a strong soldier of My love;
in penance to forgive you,
that sin not keep us apart;

in the Holy Eucharist to give Myself to you,
that our hearts be united more closely;
in extreme unction to prepare and cleanse your soul,
that our first meeting be more glorious;
in matrimony to unite man and woman,
that their union be sanctified in grace;
in holy orders to consecrate "other Christs,"
that My work on earth be continued.
These are the seven sacraments of My Church,
the seven channels of My grace:
My Church, My grace,
given that I might live in you more abundantly.

Baptism

May almighty God, the Father of our Lord Jesus
Christ, who has caused you to be born again by
water and the Holy Spirit, and granted you remission of all your sins, Himself anoint you with the
chrism of salvation in the same Christ Jesus, our
Lord, to eternal life. Amen.   Lefebvre

Confirmation

Almighty, everlasting God, who has seen fit to re-
generate these Your servants by water and the Holy
Spirit, and has given them remission of all their sins;
send forth upon them from heaven Your sevenfold
Holy Spirit, the Paraclete. Amen.

The Spirit of wisdom and understanding. Amen.

The Spirit of counsel and fortitude. Amen.

The Spirit of knowledge and piety. Amen.

Fill them with the spirit of Your holy fear and
sign them with the sign of the cross of Christ in
mercy to eternal life, through the same Jesus Christ
. . . in the unity of the same Holy Spirit, God, world
without end. Amen.   Lefebvre

Penance

May the almighty and merciful God grant you indulgence, absolution, and remission of all your sins. May our Lord Jesus Christ absolve you; and by His authority I absolve you from every bond of excommunication, suspension, and interdict, in proportion to my power and your need. Thereupon, I absolve you from your sins, in the name of the Father and of the Son and of the Holy Spirit. Amen.

May the Passion of our Lord Jesus Christ, the merits of the Blessed Virgin Mary and of all the saints, whatever good you shall have done, and evil you shall have endured, be to you for a remission of sins, increase of grace and reward of eternal life. Amen. *Lefebvre*

Holy Eucharist

Who the day before He suffered took bread into His holy and venerable hands and with His eyes lifted up to heaven, to You, God, His almighty Father, giving thanks to You, He blessed, broke, and gave it to His disciples, saying: Take and eat of this, *for this is My body.*

In like manner, after He had supped, taking also this excellent chalice into His holy and venerable hands and giving thanks to You, He blessed, and gave to His disciples, saying: Take and drink all of this, *for this is the chalice of My blood, of the new and eternal testament; the mystery of faith which shall be shed for you and for many, for the remission of sins.*

As often as you shall do these things, you shall do them in remembrance of Me.

May the body of our Lord Jesus Christ preserve my soul to life everlasting. Amen. *Lefebvre*

Extreme Unction

In the name of the Father and of the Son and of the Holy Spirit, let there be extinguished in you all power of the devil by the imposition of our hands, and by the invocation of all holy angels, archangels, patriarchs, prophets, apostles, martyrs, confessors, virgins, and of all the saints. Amen.

O Lord Jesus Christ, let there enter this house with the entrance of our lowliness eternal happiness, divine prosperity, serene gladness, fruitful charity, everlasting health; may there fly from this place all approach of the demons; let the angels of peace be present and all ill-feeling and discord leave this house. Make Your name great over us, O Lord, and bless our ministry: hallow the entrance of our lowliness, You who are holy, You who are kind, and abide with the Father and Holy Spirit, world without end. Amen.   Lefebvre

Matrimony

May the God of Abraham, the God of Isaac, and the God of Jacob be with you, and may He fulfill His blessing in you; that you may see your children's children even to the third and fourth generation, and thereafter may you have life everlasting, by the grace of our Lord Jesus Christ, who with the Father and the Holy Spirit lives and reigns, God for ever and ever. Amen.   Lefebvre

Holy Orders

Receive the yoke of the Lord; for His yoke is sweet and His burden light.

Receive the priestly vestment, by which charity is signified; for God is powerful to increase in you charity and perfection of work.

7

Be pleased, O Lord, to consecrate and sanctify these hands by this anointing and blessing that whatsoever they shall bless may be blessed, and whatsoever they shall consecrate be consecrated and sanctified, in the name of our Lord Jesus Christ.

Receive the power to offer sacrifice to God and to celebrate Mass for the living as well as for the dead, in the name of the Lord. Amen.

Receive the Holy Spirit; whose sins you shall forgive, they are forgiven them; and whose sins you shall retain, they are retained.   Author unknown

Psalm 150

Praise the Lord in his sanctuary, praise him in his majestic firmament.

Praise him for his mighty deeds, praise him for his supreme majesty.

Praise him with the blast of the horn, praise him with harp and lyre.

Praise him with timbrel and dance, praise him with strings and pipe.

Praise him with loud-sounding cymbals, praise him with crashing cymbals: let every being that breathes praise the Lord!

The Canticle of the Sun

O most high, almighty, good Lord God, to You belong praise, glory, honor, and all blessing.

Praised be my Lord God with all His creatures, and especially our brother the sun, who brings us the day and who brings us the night; fair is he and shines with a very great splendor; O Lord, he signifies You to us.

Praised be my Lord for our sister the moon, and for the stars, which He has set clear and lovely in heaven.

Praised be my Lord for our brother the wind, and for the air, and clouds, calms and all weather by which You uphold life in all creatures.

Praised be my Lord for our sister water, who is very serviceable to us and humble and precious and very clean.

Praised be my Lord for our brother fire, through whom You give us light in the darkness; he is bright and pleasant and very mighty and strong.

Praised be my Lord for our mother the earth, which sustains us and keeps us, and brings forth grass and divers fruits and flowers of many colors.

Praise and bless the Lord, and give thanks to Him and serve Him with great humility.

Saint Francis of Assisi

The Cherubicon Prayer from the Byzantine Rite

O King of glory, no one is worthy to come to You, to draw near to You, to perform a service for You when he is bound down by desires and pleasures of the flesh; ¶ for to serve You is something grand and awe-inspiring even for the heavenly powers themselves. ¶ And yet, because of Your ineffable and boundless love for mankind, You became man without changing or diminishing Your divinity, and You became our high priest; and acting as master of all creation You granted to us the sacred power of offering up this public sacrifice without any new shedding of blood. ¶ For You alone, O Lord our God, are master over all things in heaven and on earth— ¶ You who are borne upon the throne of the cherubim, You who are the Lord of the seraphim and King of Israel, You alone are holy and rest among the holy. ¶ Still I make my prayers to You, who alone are good and graciously ready to hear me. ¶ Turn Your eyes upon me, Your sinful and unprofitable servant, and cleanse my soul and heart from any thought of evil. ¶ By the power of the Holy Spirit, render me also worthy. ¶ And so it is to You that I come with my head bowed low and beseech You not to turn away Your face from us, but to allow these gifts to be offered to You by me, Your sinful and unworthy servant; ¶ for it is really You who offers and are offered, You who receives the offering and are given back to us, Christ our God— and to You we render glory, with Your eternal Father, and with Your most holy and gracious and life-giving Spirit, now and ever and for ages of ages. Amen.   Author unknown

Oblation

O God, who in a wonderful manner did create and ennoble human nature, and still more wonderfully has renewed it; grant that by the mystery of this water and wine, we may be made partakers of His divinity who saw fit to become partaker of our humanity, Jesus Christ Your Son, our Lord: who lives and reigns with You in the union of the Holy Spirit, one God, world without end. Amen.
                                        Lefebvre

Finding God in the Mirror of Creation

Lord, I have often felt that if only I could see You, I would love You with all my heart and soul. I feel that the reason I seem to love creatures more than You is that I can see them, I can feel them, I can

10

touch them. But I cannot see, feel, or touch You. Perhaps I have not looked far enough; for if I looked around me, it is true, I would not see You, but I would see a reflection of You in Your creatures.

In the full and open blue sky, in the varicolored plumage of autumn, in the green verdure of early spring, in the face of one I love, in a whitecapped stretch of sea, in a crimson and gold sunset, in a moonlit, star-filled sky, I can see Your beauty.

In the music of the wind brushing through the trees, in the roar of the surf on the shore, in the sweeping themes of a symphony, in the soft patter of rain on my roof, in the pleasant voice of a dear one, I can hear Your beautiful voice.

In the soft fresh greenness of grass, in the gentle caress of a spring breeze, in the hard, smooth finish of a masterpiece of wood, in the plush petals of the rose, I can feel Your beautiful presence.

In the intoxicating breath of newly mown hay, in the delicious odor of early spring, in the satisfying smell of cooking food, in the full-blown scent of the wild rose, I can sense Your fragrance.

In the sweet red apple fresh from the branch, in wild honey, in fresh berries, I can taste how sweet is the Lord.

Lord, it is true I cannot see You, but I can clearly see Your reflection in the mirror of Your creation. Amen.

Late Have I Loved You

Late have I loved You, O beauty ever ancient, ever new! Late have I loved You! ¶ And behold, You were within, and I without, and without I sought You. ¶ And deformed I ran after those forms of beauty You have made. ¶ You were with me, and I was not with You, those things held me back from

You, things whose only being was to be in You. ¶ You called; You cried; and You broke through my deafness. ¶ You flashed; You shone; and You chased away my blindness. ¶ You became fragrant; and I inhaled and sighed for You. ¶ I tasted, and now hunger and thirst for You. ¶ You touched me; and I burned for Your embrace.   Saint Augustine

A Christian's Oblation

Give me Your grace, good God, not to value the opinion of the world, to fasten my mind rather on You; ¶ not to be governed by the criticism of men, to be content to be alone; ¶ not to desire worldly company, to deem the world a mere trifle, to rid my mind of all its affairs; ¶ not to long to have and possess worldly things, and that the possession of the baubles of the world may be even unpleasant to me. ¶ Let me gladly think of God, let me lean on His comfort, let me labor constantly to love Him. ¶ I pray to know my own smallness and wretchedness, ¶ to make myself humble and meek beneath the mighty hand of God, ¶ to bewail the sins I have committed, ¶ to rid myself of them by patiently bearing adversities, happy to suffer my purgatory here on earth, ¶ to be joyous in tribulation, ¶ to walk the narrow way that leads to life, ¶ to bear the cross together with Christ, ¶ to recall that this life is to end, that death is always near at hand—May death never become a stranger to me! ¶ Give me the grace to ponder the everlasting fire of hell, ¶ to pray for pardon now before I meet You, my God, as judge, ¶ to have continually in mind Christ's Passion—suffered for me— ¶ to give Him unceasing thanks for His kindness, ¶ to buy back the time that I have lost, not to waste any more time in aimless talk about worldly wealth, friends, liberty, life, ¶ to be convinced that the loss of all these things is but a slight cost for the winning of Christ, ¶ to think my greatest enemies my best friends, for their malice and hatred will frequently do me more good than would their love and favor, as was so very true with Joseph and his brothers. ¶ This state of mind, these attitudes must be more dear to us than the entire wealth of the world, even if it were gathered and laid at our feet. Amen.   Saint Thomas More

Privileges
I beg of Thee grace wherewith to enter into the depths of my privileges,—to enjoy what I possess—to believe in, to use, to improve, to glory in my present gifts as a member of Christ, child of God and inheritor of the kingdom of heaven. Amen.
                                        Cardinal Newman

Prayer for the Angels' Protection
O God, who through Your unspeakable goodness has given us Your holy angels to be our protectors, grant that we may be defended by their protection and arrive at the enjoyment of eternal good in their company. Amen.

Prayer to the Guardian Angel
Angel of God, my guardian dear,
   To whom His love commits me here;
Ever this day be at my side,
   To light and guard, to rule and guide. Amen.
                              [300 days, R. 452]

To the Holy Angel of Christ's Agony
O holy Angel who strengthened Jesus Christ our Lord, come and strengthen us also; do not delay.
                              [300 days, R. 454]

13

Bless the Lord

Bless the Lord, all you His angels; you that are mighty in strength, and execute His word. Bless the Lord, all you His hosts; you ministers of His that do His will. [300 days, R. 441]

Invocation to Saint Michael the Archangel

Saint Michael, first champion of the kingship of Christ, pray for us. [300 days, R. 443]

Prayer to Saint Raphael the Archangel

Grant, O Lord God, to send to our assistance Saint Raphael the Archangel; and may he, who, we believe, evermore stands before the throne of Your majesty, offer to You our humble petitions to be blessed by You, through Christ our Lord. Amen.

[3 years, R. 451]

Prayer to Saint Gabriel the Archangel

O God, who among all the angels did choose the Archangel Gabriel to announce the mystery of Your Incarnation; mercifully grant, that we who solemnly keep his feast on earth may feel the benefit of his patronage in heaven, who lives and reigns for ever and ever. Amen. [3 years, R. 449]

*This is the order of salvation and of sanctification
in the Church: through the Holy Spirit we
possess the Son, and through the Son, we
ascend to the Father.*
Saint Irenaeus

The Blessed Trinity

I have come that you may have life
and have it more abundantly.
The life I give you is a share of My own life,
a true share in the life of the Blessed Trinity.
The life My Father and I enjoy with the Holy Spirit
is yours
because We love you.
The Father, because He loved you, created you;
I, the Son, because I love you, redeemed you;
the Holy Spirit, because He loves you, sanctifies you
    with His grace.

As long as your soul is clothed with sanctifying grace
you are the temple of the Holy Spirit.
The three Divine Persons are truly present in you.
If any man love Me, he will keep My word
and My Father will love him.
We will come and make Our abode with him.

This life of grace you have from the Blessed Trinity
is a pure gift.
It came to you in baptism.
All power in heaven and earth has been given to Me.
Go, therefore, and make disciples of all nations,
baptizing them in the name of the Father,
and of the Son, and of the Holy Spirit.

The mystery of the Blessed Trinity
is the greatest mystery of your faith.
My mission on earth was to reveal to men the Father,
My heavenly Father who is also your Father.
I came to teach you to know and love the Father.
For this He sent Me, His divine Son,
to teach you the way,
the truth,
and the life.
No one comes to the Father but through Me.
I am the way, the truth, and the life.

If you follow Me,
it is because My Father has called you.
No man can come to Me unless My Father draws him.
But do not fear, for the Father Himself loves you.
I have prayed that the Father may love you as
    He loves Me,
that the love with which He loves Me may be in you.

You are My brothers,
you are the adopted sons of God the Father.
The apostles grieved when I ascended into heaven,
but I have asked the Father
and He has sent the Holy Spirit to be with you.
And wherever the Spirit is,
there also are the Father and the Son.
We have made your heart Our home.

You are the temples of the living God.
What holiness this truth should inspire you to attain,
what cleanness of both body and mind,
what reverence and love for one another.

Your life as a Christian is a real challenge.
It is a life which must be lived by faith.

But to live by faith today is not easy
because the modern world is so materialistic.
Man is taught to believe only in those things
which can be measured.
Man today wants to see, feel, and weigh everything.
Only those things which he can put in a test tube
    and analyze are real to him.
That is why many today refuse to believe in the
    Blessed Trinity.

Because these sayings are hard to believe
men of the world turn away from Me.
But you have been given the gift of faith,
the grace to believe the truths I revealed;
and by exercising this gift of faith
you will become holy
as your heavenly Father is holy
because the just man lives by faith.

Your challenge today is to meet the attack on
    your faith.
To meet this challenge in your devotional life
you must cultivate in your soul a deep spirit of faith
and a solid devotion to the Blessed Trinity dwelling
    in you.
It is by faith alone that you know the Blessed Trinity;
the very foundation of the life of grace in your soul.
All other devotions should build upon a great love
of the Blessed Trinity.

Faith
is to believe on the word of God,
what we do not see:
its reward
is to see and enjoy what we believe.

Saint Augustine

The Apostles' Creed

I believe in God, the Father almighty, Creator of heaven and earth; and in Jesus Christ, His only Son, our Lord; who was conceived by the Holy Spirit, born of the Virgin Mary, suffered under Pontius Pilate, was crucified, died, and was buried. He descended into hell, the third day He rose again from the dead. He ascended into heaven, sits at the right hand of God the Father almighty; from thence He shall come to judge the living and the dead. I believe in the Holy Spirit, the holy Catholic Church, the communion of saints, the forgiveness of sins, the resurrection of the body, and life everlasting. Amen.

[5 years, R. 43]

Act of Faith

O my God, I firmly believe that You are one God in three Divine Persons, Father, Son, and Holy Spirit. I believe that Your divine Son became man and died for our sins, and that He will come to judge the living and the dead. I believe these and all the truths which the holy Catholic Church teaches, because You have revealed them, who can neither deceive nor be deceived.

[3 years, R. 36]

Act of Hope

O my God, relying on Your almighty power and infinite mercy and promises, I hope to obtain the pardon of my sins, the help of Your grace, and life everlasting through the merits of Jesus Christ, my Lord and Redeemer.

[3 years, R. 36]

Act of Love

O my God, I love You above all things with my whole heart and soul, because You are all good and

18

worthy of all love. I love my neighbor as myself for the love of You. I forgive all who have injured me and ask pardon of all whom I have injured.

[3 years, R. 36]

Almighty and Everlasting God

Almighty and everlasting God, who has given to us Your servants grace by the profession of the true faith, to acknowledge the glory of the eternal Trinity, and, in the power of Your divine Majesty, to worship the Unity; we beseech You, that by our steadfastness in this same faith, we may evermore be defended from all adversities, through Christ our Lord. Amen.

[5 years, R. 49]

Prayer of the Angel of Fatima

My God, I believe, I adore, I hope, and I love You. I beg pardon for those who believe not, adore not, hope not, and love You not.   Barthas and Fonseca

Divine Praises

Blessed be

God.

His holy name.

Jesus Christ, true God and true man.

the name of Jesus.

His most Sacred Heart.

Jesus in the most holy Sacrament of the Altar.

the great Mother of God, Mary, most holy.

her holy and immaculate conception.

her glorious assumption.

the name of Mary, virgin and mother.

Saint Joseph, her most chaste spouse.

God in His angels and in His saints.

[3 years, R. 696]

Consecration of Saint Francis de Sales

I vow and consecrate to God all that is in me: my
memory and my actions to God the Father; my understanding and my words to God the Son; my will
and my thoughts to God the Holy Spirit; my heart,
my body, my tongue, my senses, and all my sorrows
to the sacred humanity of Jesus Christ, "who was
contented to be betrayed into the hands of wicked
men and to suffer the torment of the cross."

[3 years, R. 56]

---

*Behold what manner of love the Father has
bestowed upon us, that we should be called
children of God; and such we are.*
1 John 3:1

✝ *God the Father*

When I walked the earth I had only one mission,
to do the will of My Father who sent Me.
His will was that I teach men the way to the Father.
His will was that I give men the great gift of grace:
for grace makes you a member of God's family,
for grace makes you My brother,
for grace makes you a child of My Father.

Whenever I wished to teach men about their
    relations to God,
I did so with infinite tenderness
in the simple and intimate word
father.

20

The Old Testament
emphasized the power and justice of God;
men learned to serve their Father out of fear.
But He wanted to show mercy to them
and to be loved by them.
That is why He told you that He loved you with an
    everlasting love.

God, your Father, so loved the world as to give
    His Son.
He gave Me to each one of you.
Does this not convince you of your Father's love?
He wished to redeem you from sin,
to save you from hell, to lead you to heaven.
For this did I come into the world.

Your Father loves you and wishes to be loved by you.
He wants to help you in everything that you do,
but He waits for you to ask and call to Him for help.
You must learn to pray to the Father.

Forty days I was in the desert praying to the Father.
Only then did I begin My public teaching.
Before I chose My apostles I prayed to the Father.
At the Last Supper I prayed to the Father.
Only then did I begin My Passion.

In My Agony in the Garden
I prayed three times to the Father.
I needed His help;
I wished to set you an example.
There will be times when you too will need His help:
in choosing a state of life,
in time of temptation.
In all situations beg your heavenly Father for help.
Your Father knows your needs before you ask.

In this manner therefore shall you pray:
Our Father,
who art in heaven,
hallowed be Thy name;
Thy kingdom come;
Thy will be done on earth as it is in heaven.
Give us this day our daily bread;
and forgive us our trespasses
as we forgive those who trespass against us.
And lead us not into temptation,
but deliver us from evil. Amen.

As I told the Samaritan woman at the well,
the true adorers will worship the Father
in spirit and in truth,
for the Father also seeks such to worship Him.
God is spirit,
and they who worship Him
must worship in spirit and in truth.
No one has seen the Father except Me, His Son,
but I have revealed Him to you,
and you have received the grace to accept My word.
Therefore you are called "the sons of God."

This is the will of God—your sanctification.
My food, while I was on earth,
    was to accomplish the will of My Father.
This must be the food which nourishes your souls,
the will of your Father.
In everything you do—
your studies,
your work,
your prayer,
your recreation—
you must ask yourself:
how would a child of so good a Father act?

how would God want me to do this?
Then act with the joy of heart of a child of God.
This spirit of childlike trust and confidence in God
   your Father should characterize your whole life.
As you live so shall you die.
My last words from My cross were spoken to
   My Father:
Father, into Your hands I commend My spirit.

When men have crucified you
   because you show your love for the Father,
when you have tried to do your duty as best you can
   with no apparent success,
when the world seems to have conquered and your
   faith appears vain,
when even the Father seems to have abandoned you
   on your cross—
if you have learned the lesson taught by My life,
you too will cry out with Me,
Father, into Your hands I commend My spirit.

Your last prayer at night,
should be this same abandonment to your Father.
Then you may rest
secure in the strength of His love.

A Son to God the Father

Like any father, You expect great things of this son
of Yours; save me from being a halfhearted son.
Give me the manliness, the reverence, the loyalty of
love I need to live up to Your expectations. Make
me manly—kind and gentle, but unswayed by the
crowd and uncompromising with sin. Teach me respect—especially respect for myself; I need self-
respect to learn to reverence You in Yourself and in

others. And make me loyal, unafraid to show men by my conduct that I love You more than my very life. In a word, Father, make me another Christ. Amen.

Prayer to God the Father

My Father, You are so great, I am so little. ¶ You are the first and the last, the beginning and the end, almighty, everlasting, and yet my Father. ¶ You made me, the creature that I am, with my powers and my weaknesses, because You wanted me, even me. ¶ You put me here, You gave me this state of life, You want me back. ¶ I want to be Yours, I want to do Your work, when the end comes I want to go to You, but without You I cannot. ¶ You will not fail me, You cannot fail me: let me not fail You. ¶ I know my weakness, I have learnt it from my falls, which You have permitted, that I might learn. Is it necessary to be taught more? ¶ I can do nothing of myself, I cannot desire to do anything. ¶ I cannot keep from harm, I cannot want to keep from harm. ¶ Help me that I may, help me that I may desire it, give me the desire of sacrifice, at least the desire of the desire, I am an infant asking for bread, will my Father give me a stone?   Archbishop Goodier

Offering of Saint Thérèse

In order that I may be a living act of perfect love, I offer myself as a whole burnt offering to Your tender love, beseeching You to consume me continually, letting my soul overflow with the floods of infinite tenderness that are found in You, that so I may become a martyr of Your love, O my God! Let this martyrdom make me ready to appear before You and at last cause me to expire; let my soul cast itself without delay into the everlasting arms of Your merciful love. With every beat of my heart I desire, O my dearly Beloved, to renew this offering an infinite number of times, until that day when the shadows shall vanish and I shall be able to retell my love in an eternal face-to-face with You!

[3 years, R. 57]

As Their Father

All below heaven changes: spring, summer, autumn, each has its turn. The fortunes of the world change; what was high, lies low; what was low, rises high. Riches take wing and flee away; bereavements happen. Friends become enemies, and enemies friends. Our wishes, aims and plans change. There is nothing stable but Thee, O my God! And Thou art the center and life of all who change, who trust Thee as their Father, who look to Thee and are content to put themselves into Thy hands. Amen.

Cardinal Newman

Then said I, 'Behold, I come—(in the head of the book it is written of me)—to do thy will, O God.'
Hebrews 10:7

✝ ## God the Son

The high priest said to Me,
"I adjure You by the living God that You tell us
    whether You are the Christ, the Son of God."
I answered that I was.
I am the Son of God.

The purpose of My life was to reveal My Father
and by grace to bring men back into God's family.
I have taught you to know God, your Father.
I have won for you the gift of sanctifying grace,
that grace which makes you a child of God.
I died for each one of you on the cross,
just as My Father willed,
to show you how much I loved the Father,
to show you how much the Father loved you,
to win for you adoption into God's family.
God so loved the world that He sent Me,
His only-begotten Son.

I am the good shepherd, you are My sheep.
I know mine and mine know Me
because the Father has given you to Me,
because the Father has revealed Me to you.
And I lay down My life for My sheep,
for each one I died on the cross.

Other sheep I have that are not of this fold.
Them also I must bring into My fold,

but I need your help to reach them.
Your apostolate brings you into contact with them.
By your kindness, gentleness, and understanding
you must bring them all to Me.
They shall hear My voice
because I shall speak to them through you.
You will be My lips and My hands and My feet.
Then there will be one fold and one shepherd.

All whom the Father gives Me shall come to Me.
You have heard My call and have answered it.
You have heard My challenge and have answered it.
You shall not hunger or thirst.
You shall enter with Me into My glory with
    the Father.
Yours is life everlasting.

I have revealed the Father to you,
His love for you,
His plan for you.
I have died for you on the cross
to prove My love for the Father,
to prove My love for you.
For this reason the Father loves Me,
because I lay down My life to take it up again.
No one takes it from Me but I lay it down of Myself.
I have the power to lay it down
and the power to take it up again.
Such is the command I received from My Father.

I have asked the Father to send you the Holy Spirit
to strengthen you in your faith,
to comfort you in trials and temptations,
to sanctify you.
I have won for you the gift of grace.
What will you do for Me?

For the Friendship of Christ

I come to You, Christ my Lord, as the men of Your times came to You, attracted by Your irresistible personality. I come seeking Your friendship.

I seek You as a friend in whom I can confide when I am discouraged, confused, in need of help.

I seek You as a friend with whom I can share my hopes, my joys, my ambitions, my ideals.

I seek You as a friend whom I can love, for my heart was made to love, and You are the finest, the worthiest person I could love.

I seek You as a friend who will love me in return, for I fear to be alone, and I rely on Your love.

O Christ, draw me close to Your Sacred Heart! Reveal to me the splendor of Your personality, the strength of Your love for me. Dissolve the hard shell of selfishness enclosing my heart, that it may expand with generosity toward You. Lord Jesus, make me Your friend! Amen.

Spirit of Jesus

Dear Jesus, help me to spread Thy fragrance everywhere. Flood my soul with Thy spirit and life. Penetrate and possess my whole being so utterly that all my life may be only a radiance of Thine. Shine through me and be so in me that every soul I come in contact with may feel Thy presence in my soul. Let them look up and see no longer me but only Jesus.   Cardinal Newman

Prayer to Christ for Confidence

In a world of broken promises and deceits I come to You, Lord, with a heart full of childlike faith and confidence. I trust You, Lord, in everything which You may send me—in my trials and heartaches, my

disappointments, failures, and temptations. I know
You love me even more than I can ever love myself.
I know that if I but call on You, You will hear me.
Hear me, then, Jesus. Give me Your strength and
courage and love. Armed with these I will walk
through life with a heart of joy, a mind at peace,
and a will of high resolve. Amen.

Litany of the Holy Name

Lord, have mercy on us.   *Christ, have mercy on us.*
Lord, have mercy on us. Jesus, hear us.

Jesus, graciously hear us.
God the Father of heaven,   *have mercy on us.*
God the Son, Redeemer of the world,
God the Holy Spirit,
Holy Trinity, one God,

Jesus

 Son of the living God,   *have mercy on us.*
 splendor of the Father,
 brightness of eternal light,
 king of glory,
 sun of justice,
 Son of the Virgin Mary,
 most amiable,
 most admirable,
 mighty God,
 father of the world to come,
 angel of great council,
 most powerful,
 most patient,
 most obedient,
 meek and humble of heart,
 lover of chastity,
 lover of us,
 God of peace,

Jesus
    author of life,   *have mercy on us.*
    model of virtues,
    zealous lover of souls,
    our God,
    our refuge,
    father of the poor,
    treasure of the faithful,
    good shepherd,
    true light,
    eternal wisdom,
    infinite goodness,
    our way and our life,
    joy of the angels,
    king of patriarchs,
    master of the apostles,
    teacher of the evangelists,
    strength of martyrs,
    light of confessors,
    purity of virgins,
    crown of all saints,

Be merciful,   *spare us, O Jesus.*
Be merciful,   *graciously hear us, O Jesus.*

From
    all evil,   *deliver us, O Jesus.*
    all sin,
    your wrath,
    the snares of the devil,
    the spirit of fornication,
    everlasting death,
    the neglect of Your inspirations,

Through the mystery of Your holy Incarnation,
             deliver us, O Jesus.

Through Your
    Nativity,   *deliver us, O Jesus.*
    infancy,
    most divine life,
    labors,
    Agony and Passion,
    cross and abandonment,
    faintness and weariness,
    death and burial,
    Resurrection,
    Ascension,
    institution of the most Holy Eucharist,
    joys,
    glory,

Lamb of God, who takes away the sins of the world,
spare us, O Jesus.
Lamb of God, who takes away the sins of the world,
graciously hear us, O Jesus.
Lamb of God, who takes away the sins of the world,
have mercy on us, O Jesus.
Jesus, hear us,   *Jesus, graciously hear us.*

Let us pray. O Lord Jesus Christ, who has said: Ask and you shall receive, seek and you shall find, knock and it shall be opened to you; mercifully attend to our supplications, and grant us the gift of Your divine charity, that we may ever love You with our whole heart and with all our words and deeds, and may never cease from praising You.

Make us, O Lord, to have a perpetual fear and love of Your holy name, for You never fail to help and govern those whom You bring up in Your steadfast fear and love: who lives and reigns for ever and ever. Amen.   [7 years, R. 114]

The Sacred Heart of Jesus

✝ I call you friend—
you,
My friend.
You must try to understand this profound truth:
I, Jesus Christ, call you My friend,
and give you My love.

My love singles you out,
it surrounds you,
it guards you,
it forgives you.
It is the most important thing in your life.

Do you think that love is a weak sort of thing?
My love for you is so strong
that it brought Me down from heaven,
it made Me live poor,
it made Me work and sweat,
it made Me suffer and bleed
and die
for you.
Greater love than this no one has,
that one lay down his life for his friends.

My love for you is so strong
that it crashed the barrier of death,
that it instituted the Blessed Sacrament,
so that I could be with you,

body and blood, soul and divinity,
so that I could come into your heart
to give you strength, peace, and happiness,
to give you companionship,
to give you friendship—always.
My child, give Me your heart.

My love desires the hearts and the souls of all men.
All that I have done as man,
all that I have done through My mystical body
I have done because I desire souls,
that through Me and with Me and in Me
all men may glorify My Father.

But men will not listen to Me, their best friend;
men reject My grace,
men reject My love.
Even you—to a greater or lesser extent—reject Me
by sin.
My child, put sin out of your life.
Give Me your heart.
Don't be afraid to give yourself entirely to Me—
intellect and will,
imagination, memory, senses,
eyes, ears, head, heart, hands, feet,
your whole body,
your whole soul,
your whole being.

Come to Me,
learn from Me,
for I am meek and humble of heart.
Learn to live My life.
Learn to share in My life through grace.
Try to make all your thoughts, words, and actions
worthy of being called "Christlike."

Thus do you give Me your heart.
Thus do our two hearts learn to beat as one.
Thus do you live with My life.
You become another Christ,
you become another redeemer
working with Me to save souls.

The Devotion to the Sacred Heart

The devotion to the Sacred Heart of Jesus is the consecration of one's whole life to the Sacred Heart as a return of love and reparation. The Morning Offering is the crystallized formula for renewing this consecration every day and is the formula used by millions of souls throughout the entire world who are devoted to the Sacred Heart.

Consecration

Christ's Heart wants my soul, wants me. I give Him my soul and myself by my consecration of myself to the Sacred Heart. You know what consecration means in the Mass. The priest takes the host into his hands, bends over it, and says the words of consecration. Instantly that host ceases to be bread and is changed into Christ. Then the priest takes the chalice filled with wine. Again he says the words of consecration. Instantly the wine ceases to be wine and is changed into Christ.

When I consecrate myself to the Sacred Heart, I am also, so to speak, changed into Christ. Of course there are vast differences between this personal consecration and consecration in the Mass. In the Mass the change from bread and wine into Christ is instantaneous and complete; but in my personal consecration there is no instantaneous change, and the change will never be complete. When I say my words of consecration over myself I am only making a beginning. My consecration is a pledge that I will work at the business of changing myself into Christ. It is a promise that I will try to make every thought and word and deed of mine such that

34

Christ would gladly call it His own. It is a promise that I will try perseveringly to make myself another Christ, whose divine life I already participate in through grace. Do I see how completely I give myself to Christ through consecration seriously undertaken?

But the Heart of Christ does not stop with the desire of my soul. He desires also the souls of all other men, and if I am interested in His Heart's desire I must be interested in bringing those other souls to Him.

I do my best work of winning souls for the Sacred Heart by attending seriously to the living of my life of consecration. If I am serious about my consecration to the Sacred Heart, I am earnestly trying to make myself as Christlike as I can. I am trying to be as fully as possible another Christ. And insofar as I am truly another Christ, I am another redeemer—that is, my little works are joined with the mighty redeeming works of the Savior Himself in the ever-continuing effort for the salvation of souls.

I must not underestimate the power and the importance of my part in Christ's work of redemption. In His loving providence He has decreed that the members of His mystical body share in His work. By the incomparable labors of His life and death Christ won graces in abundance for the salvation of souls. But it remains for us, the members of His mystical body, to share in the task of applying those graces to the souls that need them, through our work in union with Him. As Pius XII in *Mystici Corporis* said: "the salvation of many depends on the prayers and voluntary penances which the faithful members of the Mystical Body of Jesus Christ offer for this intention."

Reparation

By consecration to the Sacred Heart I give our Lord my own soul and also bring to Him the souls of others. What I must notice now is that this bringing of souls— my own and those of others—is really the finest reparation I can offer to the Sacred Heart.

The word "reparation" is connected with the word "repair." When I make reparation I repair something. I make amends for a wrong. When I make reparation to the Sacred Heart I make amends to Christ for all the bitter sorrow of the Sacred Heart. What caused the great sorrow of the Sacred Heart? It was the numbing realization that the graces of redemption would be rejected by so many souls. Every sin is to a greater or lesser extent a rejection of the grace won for us by Christ. In the Agony in the Garden a deluge of sin and a deluge of rejection swept over the Savior. Redemption rejected by so many souls! The fruits of His great work thrown away! Is it any wonder that He was crushed to the earth in a bloody sweat?

By my life of consecration—or, more properly, by my life of reparation through consecration—I do all that I can to make the graces of redemption as fruitful as possible in my own soul and in the souls of as many others as I can. This is the finest reparation I can offer to the Sacred Heart of Jesus.

Our Lord Himself invented and gave to us a symbol which sets forth all the truths of devotion to the Sacred Heart. It is His Heart, bursting with flames, surmounted by a cross, wounded, crowned with thorns:

The divine Heart
　　is a symbol of His love.
The flames
　　burst forth like His love which
　　His Heart could not contain.
The wound
　　shows Him shedding the last drops of
　　His blood for us.
The crown of thorns
　　represents ingratitude, rejection, sin
　　for which we offer reparation.

The Apostleship of Prayer

The Apostleship of Prayer, which is sometimes called the League of the Sacred Heart, has been praised by the popes as "the perfect form of devotion to the Sacred Heart." It is the perfect form of the devotion because it concerns itself entirely with the life of apostolic reparation through consecration.

The great desire of the Sacred Heart is the desire for souls. Members of the Apostleship of Prayer make this desire their own. By their consecration of themselves, daily renewed, they give all their prayers, works, joys, and sufferings—everything they do—to our Lord for the intentions of His Sacred Heart. The intentions of the Sacred Heart are specified and particularized for them from month to month by Christ's vicar. The intentions are always reducible to this intention: "For the salvation of souls." The consecration of members of the Apostleship of Prayer is expressed in the Morning Offering:

O Jesus,
through the Immaculate Heart of Mary,
I offer You
all my prayers, works, joys, and sufferings
of this day
for all the intentions of Your Sacred Heart
in union
with the holy sacrifice of the Mass
throughout the world,
in reparation for my sins,
for the intentions of all our associates,
and, in particular,
for the intentions of the
holy father: . . .

To become a member of the Apostleship of Prayer you must do two things: register your name in a local center—your parish or school center if possible; promise (not under sin) to say the Morning Offering every day.

This daily recitation of the Morning Offering is the "first practice" of members of the Apostleship of Prayer. It is the only practice required of members. The "second practice" is the frequent attendance at Mass and the fervent reception of Holy Communion in a spirit of reparation at least once a month. The "third practice" is devotion to Mary through the daily recitation of at least one decade of the rosary. These last two practices, together with other acts of devotion to the Sacred Heart, are highly recommended, but are not required for membership in the Apostleship of Prayer.

"Behold this Heart,
that has loved men so much,
and in return has received
nothing but ingratitude."

Promises of Our Lord to Souls Devoted to His Sacred Heart

1 I will give them all the graces necessary in their state of life.
2 I will establish peace in their homes.
3 I will comfort them in all their afflictions.
4 I will be their secure refuge during life and above all in death.
5 I will bestow a large blessing upon all their undertakings.
6 Sinners shall find in My Heart the source and the infinite ocean of mercy.
7 Tepid souls shall grow fervent.
8 Fervent souls shall quickly mount to high perfection.
9 I will bless every place where a picture of My Heart shall be set up and honored.
10 I will give to priests the gift of touching the most hardened hearts.
11 Those who shall promote this devotion shall have their names written in My Heart never to be blotted out.
12 I promise you in the excessive mercy of My Heart that My all-powerful love will grant to all those who communicate on the first Friday in nine consecutive months the grace of final penitence; they shall not die in My disgrace nor without receiving their sacraments; My divine Heart shall be their safe refuge in this last moment.

Prayer to the Heart of Jesus

O Heart of Jesus, behold us prostrate before You, to adore You, to praise You, to thank You, to make reparation for our past faults, and to consecrate ourselves to Your love. Bearing in mind Your magnificent promises to those who honor and love Your Sacred Heart, we say to You with the utmost confidence: Heart of Jesus, give us all the graces necessary for our state of life; ¶ Heart of Jesus, grant peace to our families; ¶ Heart of Jesus, console us in our sorrows; ¶ Heart of Jesus, be our safe refuge during life, and above all at the hour of our death; ¶ Heart of Jesus, pour abundant blessings on all our labors; ¶ Heart of Jesus, be for us sinners the source and infinite ocean of mercy; ¶ Heart of Jesus, make indifferent souls fervent; ¶ Heart of Jesus, make fervent souls advance rapidly to perfection; ¶ Heart of Jesus, bless the houses where Your image is exposed and honored; ¶ Heart of Jesus, give to priests the power of touching the most hardened hearts; ¶ Heart of Jesus, . . . be our secure refuge at the last hour. Amen.   Stedman

Prayer for Love of God

O God, what will You do to conquer the fearful hardness of our hearts? Lord, You must give us new hearts, tender hearts, sensitive hearts, to replace hearts that are made of marble and of bronze.

You must give us Your own Heart, Jesus. Come, lovable Heart of Jesus. Place Your Heart deep in the center of our hearts and enkindle in each heart a flame of love as strong, as great, as the sum of all the reasons that I have for loving You, my God.

O holy Heart of Jesus, dwell hidden in my heart, so that I may live only in You and only for You, so that, in the end, I may live with You eternally in heaven. Amen.   Blessed Claude de la Colombiere

Oration of the Mass of the Sacred Heart

O God, who deigned mercifully to bestow upon us infinite treasures of love in the Heart of Your Son which was wounded for our sins; grant, we beseech You, that we who pay Him the devout homage of our piety may in like manner show to You our due of worthy satisfaction, through the same Christ our Lord. Amen.   [5 years, R. 265]

O Divine Heart

O divine Heart of Jesus, grant, I pray You, eternal rest to the souls in purgatory, the final grace to those who are about to die this day, true repentance to sinners, the light of faith to pagans, and Your blessing to me and to all who are dear to me. To You, therefore, O most merciful Heart of Jesus, I commend all those souls, and in their behalf I offer to You all Your merits in union with the merits of Your most Blessed Mother and of all the angels and saints, together with all the Masses, Communions, prayers, and good works which are this day being offered throughout Christendom.   [500 days, R. 261]

Prayer of Reparation

Lord, accept these few moments of prayer in reparation for my own indifference and the indifference of all men toward Your abundant outpouring of graces upon us. Although I so frequently forget, I want at least now to make up in some small way for all my thoughtlessness, my lack of gratitude and appreciation of Your goodness to me. But most of all, Lord, let me thank You for being so infinitely patient and understanding with me, and for always remembering me, even though I so often forget You. Amen.

Act of Consecration

I, (NAME), give and consecrate myself to the Sacred Heart of our Lord Jesus Christ. I offer my person and my life, my actions, my works, and sufferings, and it is my desire henceforth to use no part of my being save in honoring, loving, and glorifying Him. It is my steadfast purpose to belong only to Him, to do everything for love of Him, and to renounce absolutely all that could displease Him.

Therefore I take You, O Sacred Heart, as the sole object of my love, as the protector of my life, as the safeguard of my salvation, and the remedy of my frailty and fickleness; for You can make good all that I have done amiss, and You will be my sure refuge at the hour of my death.

Be, O loving Heart, my justification before God the Father, and turn aside from me His wrath that I have so justly deserved. I put all my confidence in You, for I fear my own wickedness and weakness, and hope all from Your goodness.

Destroy in me all that may displease or oppose You. Let Your pure love be so firmly impressed upon my heart that I may never forget You and never be separated from You. I implore You of Your mercy suffer my name to be inscribed on Your Heart, for I wish all my happiness and all my glory to consist in living and dying as Your slave. Amen.

Saint Margaret Mary Alacoque

Consecration of the Family to the
Sacred Heart of Jesus

O most Sacred Heart of Jesus, You revealed to Saint Margaret Mary Your desire to rule over Christian families; behold, in order to please You, we stand before You this day, to proclaim Your full sovereignty over our family. We desire henceforth to live Your life, we desire that the virtues, to which You have promised peace on earth, may flower in the bosom of our family; we desire to keep far from us the spirit of the world, which You have condemned. You are king of our minds by the simplicity of our faith; You are king of our hearts by our love of You alone, with which our hearts are on fire and whose flame we shall keep alive by frequently receiving the Holy Eucharist. Be pleased, O Sacred Heart, to preside over our gathering together, to bless our spiritual and temporal affairs, to ward off all annoyance from us, to hallow our joys and comfort our sorrows. If any of us has ever been so unhappy as to fall into the misery of displeasing You, grant that he may remember, O Heart of Jesus, that You are full of goodness and mercy toward the repentant sinner. And when the hour of separation strikes and death enters our family circle, whether we go or whether we stay, we shall all bow humbly before Your eternal decrees. This shall be our consolation, to remember that the day will come when our entire family once more united in heaven shall be able to sing of Your glory and Your goodness forever. May the Immaculate Heart of Mary and the glorious patriarch Saint Joseph offer You this, our act of consecration, and keep the memory of it in us all the days of our lives. Glory to the Heart of Jesus, our King and our Father! [R. 705]

Litany of the Sacred Heart

Lord, have mercy on us.   *Christ, have mercy on us.*
Lord, have mercy on us. Christ, hear us.
                              Christ, graciously hear us.
God the Father of heaven,   *have mercy on us.*
God the Son, Redeemer of the world,
God the Holy Spirit,
Holy Trinity, one God,

Heart of Jesus
   Son of the eternal Father,   *have mercy on us.*
   formed by the Holy Spirit in the womb
      of the Virgin Mother,
   substantially united to the Word of God,
   of infinite majesty,
   sacred temple of God,
   tabernacle of the Most High,
   house of God and gate of heaven,
   burning furnace of charity,
   abode of justice and love,
   full of goodness and love,
   abyss of all virtues,
   most worthy of all praise,
   king and center of all hearts,
   in whom are all the treasures of wisdom
      and knowledge,
   in whom dwells the fullness of divinity,
   in whom the Father is well pleased,
   of whose fullness we have all received,
   desire of the everlasting hills,
   patient and most merciful,
   enriching all who invoke You,
   fountain of life and holiness,
   propitiation for our sins,
   loaded down with opprobrium,
   bruised for our offenses,

Heart of Jesus
 obedient even to death,   *have mercy on us.*
 pierced with a lance,
 source of all consolation,
 our life and resurrection,
 our peace and reconciliation,
 victim of sin,
 salvation of those who hope in You,
 hope of those who die in You,
 delight of all the saints,

Lamb of God, who takes away the sins of the world,
         spare us, O Lord.
Lamb of God, who takes away the sins of the world,
       graciously hear us, O Lord.
Lamb of God, who takes away the sins of the world,
        have mercy on us.
Jesus, meek and humble of heart,
      make our hearts like Yours.

Let us pray. O almighty and eternal God, look upon the Heart of Your dearly beloved Son and upon the praise and satisfaction He offers You in behalf of sinners, and being appeased grant pardon to those who seek Your mercy, in the name of the same Jesus Christ Your Son, who lives and reigns with You, in the unity of the Holy Spirit, world without end. Amen.   [7 years, R. 245]

The Way of the Cross

The Way of the Cross can be an excellent form of mental prayer and an excellent way to rouse in ourselves a sense of sorrow for sin and love for our Lord whom sin has offended.

A plenary indulgence may be gained each time the Way of the Cross is made, and a second plenary indulgence is gained if the person has received Holy Communion on the same day. All that is required to gain the indulgence is that the person walk from station to station and pause before each one to meditate on the sufferings of our Lord. No vocal prayers need be said. The method here suggested consists merely in presenting appropriate thoughts which may help the person in his meditation upon these sacred mysteries.

FIRST STATION: Jesus is condemned to death.

Picture our Lord in bloodstained garments standing with bowed head before Pilate, the Roman governor.

Consider the outrage as the Master of life and death hears the death sentence passed against Him and hears the mob yell for the murderer Barabbas in preference to Himself; the suffering of the mystical Christ, as He stands on trial today in the courtrooms of Russia and China in the persons of His persecuted priests, religious, and faithful laymen.

Reflect upon your own willingness to stand up for what you know is right, even though it may mean incurring the condemnation of others.

After reflection speak trustfully with our Lord, who for love of you allows Himself to be condemned to death.

SECOND STATION: Jesus takes up His cross.

Picture the weary arms of our Lord as He accepts the cross from the hands of His executioners.

Consider the utter weariness of His body after a night of mockery and torture; the utter dread within His soul as He foresees the sufferings which still await Him; the suffering caused to the mystical Christ by the lukewarm Christians who rebel at suffering, who refuse to bear their cross for the salvation of men, and demand that God take the cross out of their lives.

Reflect upon your own attitude toward suffering, accepting it from God's hand as a means of your own salvation and that of your neighbor.

After reflection speak trustfully with our Lord, who for love of you takes up this heavy burden.

45

THIRD STATION: Jesus falls the first time.

Picture the bruised body of our Lord thrust to the ground by the weight of the cross.

Consider the pain which this jolt intensifies in His wounded body; the sense of shame and helplessness and infinite sorrow for their ignorance as He falls at the feet of His tormentors; the pain caused the mystical Christ by the falls of Christians into sin, especially public sins and scandal.

Reflect upon your own attitude toward sin and your attempts to overcome your weaknesses effectively, especially the one which seems to be the root of your sins.

After reflection speak trustfully with our Lord, who for love of you endures the pain of this fall.

FOURTH STATION: Jesus meets His Mother.

Picture our Lord as His eyes meet those of His Blessed Mother.

Consider the increase of our Lord's agony as He realizes the terrible grief His suffering is causing His Mother; Mary's tremendous pain as she sees the bloody and abused flesh, once the sweet infant of Bethlehem; how their sufferings are joined in the work of redemption; the sorrow of Mary, the mother of the human family, as she sees so many of her sons and daughters reject her and her divine Son.

Reflect upon your own devotion to Mary, and your effort to live as her true child and to go to her in all your needs.

After reflection speak trustfully with our Lord and our Lady, who for love of you share this pain.

FIFTH STATION: Simon helps Jesus carry His cross.

Picture the trembling limbs and faltering step of our Lord under His cross.

Consider a weakness so great and a pain so excruciating that the Romans fear their victim will die before reaching Calvary; the feeling of shame and rejection as our Lord hears Simon's complaint; the cold and cruel refusal of many to help the mystical Christ as He faints from hunger and shivers from cold in His poor and shelterless members today.

Reflect upon your own spirit of Christian charity and your willingness to help another carry his cross.

After reflection speak trustfully with our Lord, who for love of you has become weak and humiliated.

SIXTH STATION: Veronica wipes the face of Jesus.

Picture Veronica pressing her veil with the tenderest care to the cut, swollen, and feverish face of our Lord.

Consider the marvelous love of Veronica for our Lord as she braves the crowd to perform this act of kindness; the marvelous reward she receives in return, the impression of the blessed face of our Lord; the need in the mystical body for Christians who will offer themselves to our Lord and who in return will receive His likeness imprinted on their souls.

Reflect to see if you are a "Christopher," a Christ-bearer, and if others can see a resemblance to our Lord in your actions and attitudes.

After reflection speak trustfully with our Lord, who desires to impress His likeness on your soul, so that it be no longer you who live but Christ who lives in you.

SEVENTH STATION: Jesus falls the second time.

Picture the body of our Lord shoved roughly to the earth by the weight of the cross.

Consider the pain of this fall which reopens all His wounds; the courage which is needed to rise again in the face of certain knowledge of falls yet to come; the damage done to the mystical body of Christ by quitters, "those who set their hand to the plow and then look back"; that those who do great work for God, despite fear and failure, always rise for another try; the need for Christians who are willing to risk failure in attempting great things for the glory of God.

Reflect upon your fortitude in the face of failures and discouragement, in the face of your own inadequacy.

After reflection speak trustfully with our Lord, who for love of you courageously rises again.

EIGHTH STATION: Jesus meets the women of Jerusalem.

Picture our suffering Lord as He stops before the group of women.

Consider the boundless charity of our Lord, as He ignores His own suffering to speak to these women; His straightforward words to them; the harm done to the mystical body by those Christians who, "polite and kind," hesitate to discuss in open words the vital truths of religion and the meaning of life.

Reflect upon your own willingness to forget your own troubles for the sake of others and to face strong realities such as death, judgment, and redemption.

After reflection speak trustfully with our Lord, who gives you this example of true charity and zeal.

NINTH STATION: Jesus falls the third time.

Picture the body of our Lord wholly prostrated by an agony of weakness and pain.

Consider a weakness that is paralyzing, a pain that is crushing; the determination which is needed to crawl the last few feet to Calvary; the sins of pride in today's world which press the face of God to the dust.

Reflect upon your own willingness to submit to rightful authority and to crawl into heaven upon the knees of humility, persevering to the very end.

After reflection speak trustfully with our Lord, who for love of you has crawled the hill of Calvary.

TENTH STATION: Jesus is stripped of His garments.

Picture the raw flesh of our Lord exposed and torn anew by the stripping of His clothes.

Consider the terrible renewal of each pain as the wounds are reopened by this rough removal of their only protection; the sense of humiliation of our Lord as His sacred body is exposed to the curious gaze of the onlookers; the tearing at the garments of the mystical Christ in today's systematic conspiracy against modesty and purity; the need for Christians imbued with a militant and apostolic spirit of purity.

Reflect upon your own attitudes toward chaste living and your attempts to convey those attitudes to others.

After reflection speak trustfully with our Lord, who for love of you has willingly suffered this tremendous pain and humiliation.

ELEVENTH STATION: Jesus is nailed to the cross.

Picture the hands of our Lord willingly opened to receive the nails.

Consider the stab of pain as the nail pierces flesh and nerve; the gesture of love as the arms are outstretched to embrace the whole world, but receive in return only the blow of the nails; the terrible power of sin that can hammer God to a cross; the hammer strokes that the mystical Christ must endure every time a mortal sin is committed; the reparation and comfort that the members of the mystical body can offer Him by penance and sacrifices.

Reflect upon your own determination to avoid mortal sin at all costs; the reparation you should offer Christ for the sins being committed today.

After reflection speak trustfully with our Lord, who for love of you had rough nails driven through His sacred hands and feet.

TWELFTH STATION: Jesus dies on the cross.

Picture the torn and twisted body of our Lord; His desperate gasping for breath as the death agony sets in.

Consider the climax and totality of pain, racking every limb, tearing every muscle, stabbing every nerve; the tremendous love which inspired so great a suffering; "greater love than this no one has, that one lay down his life for his friends"; how the members of Christ's mystical body imitate His selfless love—martyrs praying for their executioners, the sick and the dying suffering without a murmur, everyday saints bearing secret crosses— what a fit response to His love!

Reflect upon your own response to His love; the kind of love Christ expects you to show Him as His Sacred Heart empties itself for love of you.

After reflection speak trustfully with our Lord, who for love of you has died upon the cross.

THIRTEENTH STATION: Jesus is taken down from the cross.

Picture the cold, lifeless, and bruised body of Christ resting in the arms of Mary.

Consider this is the result of sin; the forbidden pleasure of sin; its attractiveness tastes bitter as we watch Mary gaze at the tortured body of her Son; the mystical body of Christ is tortured by today's sins, for the mystical Christ is put on His cross every day.

Reflect upon your own awareness of the terribleness of sin; this silent sermon spoken by the mournful eyes of the Blessed Mother as she holds the body of her Son.

After reflection speak trustfully with our Lord, who for love of you felt the terrible effects of sin.

FOURTEENTH STATION: Jesus is laid in the tomb.

Picture the holy women preparing the lifeless body of Jesus for burial.

Consider the spirit of these women who stayed with our Lord to the very end and even now, in the face of the final reality of death, do not abandon Him; the faithful today who carry on works of mercy and the apostolate in the face of tremendous difficulties, but whose cry is: "my trust shall never leave me!"

Reflect upon the strength of your own trust in God, in spite of great difficulties and trials, and the need today for Christians who dare to hope for the best from God and, therefore, are willing to attempt great things for Him.

After reflection speak trustfully with our Lord, who for love of you has suffered and died.

*Do you not know that you are the temple of God
and that the Spirit of God dwells in you?*
1 Corinthians 3:16

God the Holy Spirit

And now I am going to Him who sent Me,
but because I have spoken to you these things
sadness has filled your heart.
It is expedient for you that I depart,
for if I do not go the Advocate will not come to you.
But if I go, I will send Him to you.

When the time had come for Me to depart,
to return to My Father,
My apostles were sad.
I promised them I would not abandon them.
I instituted the sacrament of My body and blood
to be with them always.
I also promised that I would send the Holy Spirit
to be their comforter.

The Advocate, the Holy Spirit,
whom the Father will send in My name,
will teach you all things
and bring to your mind
whatever I have said to you.

I have asked the Father to send you the Holy Spirit.
Your soul is the home of God
because the Holy Spirit dwells there.
If the Holy Spirit is there,
so also are the Father and I, His Son.

You are the temple of the Blessed Trinity,
the house of God.
God is not just an occasional visitor to your soul,
He dwells there.
The life of God is within you while you are in grace.
Mortal sin alone can evict the Holy Spirit from His
    home in your soul.

Devotion to the Holy Spirit is easy for you
because He is so close to you, dwelling within you.
You do not have to go to a church to find God if
    you are in the state of grace.
God abides in your heart,
He is living within you.
The Holy Spirit within you speaks to your soul.
In temptations He strengthens and inspires you
    to act as a child of God.
He inspires good thoughts in your soul
and prompts you to do what is more pleasing to God.

I came to earth to make you a child of God.
To be a true child of God you must possess the
    Holy Spirit by grace.
He will inspire you to act according to the mind
    of Christ.
Whoever is led by the Spirit of God,
he is the son of God.

You are the temple of God
and the Spirit of God dwells in you.

Prayer to God the Holy Spirit

Holy Spirit of God, love of God, silent, secret, all
preserving, breathing where you list, expressing our
longings. ¶ You are wisdom, You are love, You are

strength and fidelity; ¶ I am none of these, I need them all, sincerely I want them, I do believe sincerely I want them. ¶ You are the Father of the poor; ¶ You do not fail. ¶ Will You fail me? That I may never fail You, I cannot trust myself; ¶ that I may never do wrong; ¶ that I may be wise according to my place in life; ¶ that I may love truly, not falsely; ¶ that I may be faithful to God, to men; ¶ that I may have strength sufficient for the task you give me and may use it.   Archbishop Goodier

Come, Holy Spirit (Veni Sancte Spiritus)

Holy Spirit! Lord of light!
From Thy clear celestial height,
Thy pure, beaming radiance give.

Come, Thou, Father of the poor!
Come, with treasures which endure!
Come, Thou light of all that live!

Thou of all consolers best,
Visiting the troubled breast,
Dost refreshing peace bestow.

Thou in toil art comfort sweet;
Pleasant coolness in the heat;
Solace in the midst of woe.

Light immortal! Light divine!
Visit Thou these hearts of Thine,
And our inmost being fill.

If Thou take Thy grace away,
Nothing pure in man will stay;
All his good is turned to ill.

Heal our wounds—our strength renew;
On our dryness pour Thy dew;
Wash the stains of guilt away:

Bend the stubborn heart and will;
Melt the frozen, warm the chill;
Guide the steps that go astray;

Thou on those who evermore
Thee confess and Thee adore,
In Thy sevenfold gifts descend.

Give them comfort when they die;
Give them life with Thee on high;
Give them joys which never end. Amen.
[5 years]

Come, O Holy Spirit
Come, O Holy Spirit, replenish the hearts of Your faithful and kindle in them the fire of Your love.
Send forth Your Spirit, and they shall be created;
And You shall renew the face of the earth.

Let us pray. O God, who by the light of the Holy Spirit did instruct the hearts of the faithful, grant us by the same Spirit a love and relish of what is right and just and the constant enjoyment of His comforts, through Christ our Lord. Amen.   [5 years, R. 287]

O, Holy Spirit
O, Holy Spirit, soul of my soul, I adore You. Enlighten, guide, strengthen, and console me. Tell me what I ought to do and command me to do it. I promise to be submissive in everything that You permit to happen to me; only show me what is Your will. Amen.   Cardinal Mercier

Novena Prayer to the Holy Spirit

O Holy Spirit, divine Spirit of light and love, I consecrate to You my understanding, my heart, and my
will—my whole being for time and eternity. May my
understanding be always submissive to Your heavenly inspiration and to the teachings of the holy
Catholic Church of which You are the infallible
guide; may my heart be ever inflamed with love of
God and my neighbor; may my will be ever con-
formed to Your divine will; and may my whole life
be a faithful imitation of the life and virtues of our
Lord and Savior, Jesus Christ, to whom with the
Father and You be honor and glory forever. Amen.

[500 days, R. 289]

---

*. . . all generations shall call me blessed; because
he who is mighty has done great things
for me, and holy is his name.*
Luke 1:48-49

The Blessed Virgin Mary

Son, behold your mother.
From the hard wood of the cross
as the last act of My life
I gave My Mother to you.
Why?
Because I wanted to give you everything
I gave you My most precious treasure—
My Mother.
What joy and gratitude should be yours!

55

Mother, behold your son.
When I spoke these words
Mary took you to her heart
as her son.
My wonderful gift made us brothers.
My gift made Mary your mother.
Accept her, then, as your mother,
she who mothered your divine life,
your life of grace,
who will answer your every prayer,
loves you with a mother's love.

I have placed your soul
in My Mother's hands.
She is the mother of your life of grace.
Through her you receive the graces I won for
   you on Calvary.
She will lead you nearer to Me.

To Me, Jesus, through Mary.
This is the way of perfection for you to follow.
Your devotion to Mary
is the same in kind as that of all Christians,
but it must differ greatly in degree—
in its strength,
in its ardor,
in its depth.
You must promise to become, as Pius XII once said,
"her visible hands upon earth."

That is a challenge.

Like every good mother
Mary ambitions great things for her children.
You answer the challenge
by living up to Mary's ambitions for you.

She desires most of all to transform you into
  another Christ through grace.
She wants to say of you,
as was once said of Me,
"This is My beloved Son, in whom I am
  well pleased."

Mary is your queen and mother.

She will protect you against the deceits of Satan,
she will strengthen you against the sinful desires
  of the flesh,
she will win grace and forgiveness for you,
should you suffer the misfortune of mortal sin,
she will give you the joy that comes from serving Me,
she will see that you persevere to the end;
for no true servant of Mary will ever be lost!

The Hail Mary
A beggar is seated at a busy street corner,
pencils and a tin cup at his side.
A young woman, child in arms, approaches.
"Good morning, ma'am."
He pays her a compliment,
"You're looking well this morning, ma'am."
And knowing a mother's heart he adds,
"What a cute youngster."
Then he glances at his cup,
he glances at his poor stump of a leg.
(Next there is the sound of a coin falling into the cup.)
"Thank you, ma'am, and God bless you."

There are other beggars, myself for instance!
I beg thus: "Hail Mary" ("Good morning").
I notice her loveliness:
"Full of grace, the Lord is with thee.
Blessed art thou among women."

And knowing that she is a mother:
"Blessed is the fruit of thy womb, Jesus."
Then conscious of my need:
"Holy Mary, Mother of God, pray for us";
and I show her my sins and faults and failings,
"sinners,"
And my misery is actual, my need is present,
"now";
and because I may not be able to beg
when I am most in need,
"and at the hour of our death. Amen."

The Rosary

The rosary as a practice of devotion to our Lady has
the highest approval of the Church and is an easy way
of meditating upon the great events in the life of Christ
and Mary. At Fatima Mary asked all Catholics to recite
the rosary frequently for the conversion of Russia and in
reparation for the sins of all men.

The ordinary indulgences which can be gained: five
years each time five decades are recited; ten years once
a day if five decades are recited with another person;
plenary for five decades before the Blessed Sacrament.

THE JOYFUL MYSTERIES

Recited every Monday and Thursday and on Sundays
from the first Sunday of Advent until the first Sunday
of Lent.

Annunciation: The good news comes to Mary. She
conceives Jesus in her womb by the power of the Holy
Spirit. Her quick and generous response: "Be it done to
me according to Your word."

Visitation: The good news comes to Elizabeth. John
the Baptist is sanctified by Mary's presence.

Nativity: The good news comes to all men. Jesus, our
Savior, is born in the cave at Bethlehem.

Presentation in the Temple: Mary offers her Son for
the service of His Father. Simeon prophesies concerning
Mary's sorrows.

*The nearer we draw to the Blessed Virgin, the
more we discover how we are strengthened
by her silent presence.*
P. Doncoeur

Finding in the Temple: After three sorrowful days
without her Son, Mary rejoices at last to find Jesus
among the teachers in the Temple.

THE SORROWFUL MYSTERIES

Recited every Tuesday and Friday and on Sundays
during Lent.

Agony in the Garden: Under the weight of men's sins,
Jesus prays, "Not My will, but Yours be done."

Scourging: Jesus feels the cutting pain inflicted by
the lash. Sins of the flesh have cut into the sacred body
of Christ.

Crowning with Thorns: The soldiers mock their king
after crowning Him with piercing thorns. They scorn His
divine authority.

Carrying of the Cross: "He is the most abject of men
. . . a worm and no man . . . yet He has borne the
iniquities of us all."

Crucifixion: "Greater love than this no one has, that
one lay down his life for his friends."

THE GLORIOUS MYSTERIES

Recited every Wednesday and Saturday and on Sundays from Easter until Advent.

Resurrection: "He has risen as He said." Jesus, the
Resurrection and the Life, appears to His friends to console and strengthen them.

Ascension: His divine mission accomplished, Jesus returns to His Father and bids us lift up our hearts.

Descent of the Holy Spirit: The Spirit of strength
and love comes down from heaven. The Catholic Church
is founded to carry on the work of Christ.

Assumption of the Blessed Virgin: The Mother of God is honored by being taken body and soul into heaven to be forever with Jesus. How great is her happiness with her divine Son!

Coronation of the Blessed Virgin: By a decree of God, Mary is crowned Queen of heaven and earth, and now distributes all graces to men on earth.

Fatima

During World War I the Blessed Virgin appeared to three shepherd children near Fatima, a town in Portugal about sixty miles from Lisbon. Her six visits began in May of 1917 and ended in October, the month of the rosary. During her conversations with the children she requested the daily recitation of the rosary, the consecration of the world to her Immaculate Heart, and Communion of reparation on the first Saturday of every month.

The Five First Saturdays

"Look, my daughter, my Heart is all pierced with thorns, which men drive into it every moment by their blasphemies and ingratitude. Do you at least seek to console me, and let men know that I promise to assist at the hour of death, with the graces necessary for salvation, all those who on the first Saturday of five consecutive months will:

1 go to confession, receive Holy Communion,
2 recite the beads,
3 and keep me company during a quarter of an hour, meditating on the fifteen mysteries of the rosary,
4 with the purpose of making reparation."

Barthas and Fonseca

The sacrament of penance must be received within an eight-day period before or after Communion. The fifteen-minute meditation may be on all or on one special mystery. The rosary and meditation may be combined by thinking on each mystery a few minutes before or after reciting the decade. A sermon for the occasion may be substituted for the meditation.

*Everyone who trusts in Mary's protection
will be saved.*
Saint Bonaventure

Fatima Prayer for Sinners

O my Jesus, forgive us our sins, save us from the
fires of hell, and bring all souls to heaven especially
those who most need Your mercy.

Barthas and Fonseca

Prayer to the Immaculate Heart
   of Mary for Holiness

Immaculate Heart of Mary, perfect model of sanctity, take my soul and mold it according to your
sublime perfections. ¶ Purify my heart and set it free
from every obstacle to holiness so that, selfless and
pure, you may adorn it with the virtues and perfections of your own Immaculate Heart. ¶ Then lead
my soul to that divine intimacy which alone can
satisfy the immense capacity for love and union with
which God has created the human heart. ¶ From you
I confidently hope for this grace of holiness and I
entrust my eternal destiny to your Immaculate
Heart. Amen.

Act of Consecration to the Immaculate
   Heart of Mary

Immaculate Heart of Mary, Queen of heaven and
earth and tender Mother of men, we humbly kneel
before your throne, and with deepest love and gratitude do this day consecrate ourselves, body and soul,
irrevocably to you. O Heart of Mary, Conqueror in
all the great battles of God, reign over us all, and
teach us how to make the Heart of Jesus reign and

61

triumph in us as it has reigned and triumphed in you. Fill our poor hearts with the great virtues that are yours, with simplicity and innocence, with meekness and courage, with fidelity and selfless love. Save us, holy Mother, from the world, from Satan and from ourselves. Watch over us and protect us so that we may belong completely to you all the days of our lives, in our joys and sorrows, in health and sickness and most of all at the moment of our death.

Most compassionate heart of Mary, with a mother's love and pity look upon the poor, sinful, suffering children of the whole human race. Remember the war-torn and the homeless and the persecuted. Do not forget the anguish you endured for them with Jesus crucified on Calvary, but by the merits of His precious blood bring them comfort in their misery. Stay the swelling flood of godless communism. Draw its leaders out of darkness and error and lead them into the light and grace of God. Grant, we beseech thee, O Mother, that peace may come once more to our world: peace to souls, peace to families, peace to our country, peace among nations. May your love and favor shine upon earth and bring to it at last the triumph of God's kingdom, so that one day all men may join their voices together in the eternal Magnificat of praise, honoring with their love and gratitude the adorable Heart of Jesus and your own Immaculate Heart. Amen.   Author unknown

Memorare

Remember, O most gracious Virgin Mary, that never was it known that anyone who fled to your protection, implored your help, or sought your intercession, was left unaided. ¶ Inspired by this confidence I fly to you, O Virgin of virgins and Mother; to you I

come, before you I stand, sinful and sorrowful;
O Mother of the Word Incarnate; despise not my
petitions, but in your mercy hear and answer me.
Amen. [3 years, R. 339]

Mary-Likeness

Mary-like in soul and body!
Mary-like in mind and heart!
Mary-like in every action—
Child of God, how fair thou art!
Fair to Christ and all His angels;
Fair to earth, since thou art seen
To be like her—like Mary,
Earth's and heaven's fairest Queen.

Night and day, in joy and sorrow,
Night and day, 'neath crushing care,
Ask of Christ true Mary-likeness—
Through the year be this thy prayer,
Christ will hear and Christ will answer
If thy pleadings but ring true:—
"Jesus, make me just like Mary,
Mary, keep me just like you."
Sisters of Providence

For Mary's Protection

We fly to your protection, O holy Mother of God,
despise not our petitions in our necessities, but deliver us always from all dangers, O glorious and
blessed Virgin. [5 years, R. 333]

The Angelus

The Angelus is said three times a day, at dawn, at noon, and at dusk, to recall the Incarnation of Christ, the great mystery by which God became man. The Angelus is a beautiful prayer in honor of Mary, for through her Christ came to us.

The angel of the Lord declared to Mary.
> *And she conceived of the Holy Spirit.*

Hail Mary.
Behold the handmaid of the Lord.
> *Be it done to me according to Your word.*

Hail Mary.
And the Word was made flesh.
> *And dwelt among us.*

Hail Mary.

Let us pray. Pour forth, we beseech You, O Lord, Your grace into our hearts; that we, to whom the Incarnation of Your Son was made known through the message of an angel, may by His Passion and cross be brought to the glory of His Resurrection, through the same Christ our Lord. Amen.

[10 years, R. 331a]

Queen of Heaven (Regina Coeli)

During Paschal time the Regina Coeli is substituted for the Angelus, to recall Mary's joy for the triumph of her Son in His Resurrection.

O Queen of heaven, rejoice, alleluia;
For He whom you did merit to bear, alleluia;
Is risen as He said, alleluia.
Pray for us to God, alleluia.
Rejoice and be glad, O Virgin Mary, alleluia.
Because our Lord is truly risen, alleluia.

Let us pray. O God, who by the Resurrection of Your Son, our Lord Jesus Christ, has been pleased to fill the world with joy, grant, we beseech You, that through the Virgin Mary, His Mother, we may receive the joy of eternal life, through the same Christ our Lord. Amen. [10 years, R. 331b]

Hail Holy Queen

Hail, holy Queen, Mother of Mercy, our life, our sweetness, and our hope. ¶ To you do we cry, poor banished children of Eve; to you do we send up our sighs, mourning and weeping in this valley of tears. ¶ Turn then, most gracious advocate, your eyes of mercy toward us, and after this our exile show us the blessed fruit of your womb, Jesus. ¶ O clement, O loving, O sweet Virgin Mary. [5 years, R. 332]

Prayer of Saint Aloysius Gonzaga

O holy Mary, my Lady, into your blessed trust and special keeping, into the bosom of your tender mercy, this day, every day of my life, and at the hour of my death, I commend my soul and body. ¶ To you I entrust all my hopes and consolations, all my trials and miseries, my life and the end of my life, ¶ that through your most holy intercession and your merits, all my actions may be ordered and disposed according to your will and that of your divine Son. Amen. [3 years, R. 343]

Prayer of Saint John Bosco

O Mary, powerful Virgin, you are the mighty and glorious protector of holy Church; ¶ you are the marvelous help of Christians; ¶ you are terrible as an army in battle array; ¶ you alone have destroyed every heresy in the whole world. ¶ In the midst of our anguish, our struggles, and our distress defend us from the power of the enemy and at the hour of our death receive our souls in paradise. Amen.

[3 years, R. 414]

Gratitude to the Blessed Mother

How can I ever begin to thank you, Mary, for the abundance of graces I have received through your hands. ¶ As a mother you have helped me in every need, comforted me in my troubles, ¶ shared my joys with me, ¶ strengthened me in temptation, ¶ counseled me in my problems, ¶ guided me along the path of virtue and purity, ¶ and taught me to know your divine Son. ¶ I will try to show my love and gratitude by making every action of my life as pleasing as possible to you, my mother, and to your divine Son. Amen.

Prayer to Mary, Our Mother

Dear Mary, my mother, you are everything that I love and admire. You are holy, you are pure, you are loving, you are kind. You are a perfect mother, Mary; help me to be a worthy child. Help me to pray when I find it hard, help me to be pure in the face of all temptations, help me to love those you love, help me to be kind to everyone. Dear Mother of God, help me with your grace to be in some small way like you so that, like you, I may some day enjoy the presence of your Son. Amen.

66

*The more sinful we are, the greater is
Mary's tenderness and pity for us.*
Curé d'Ars

Consecration to Mary

My Queen, my Mother, I give myself entirely to
you; and to show my devotion to you, I consecrate
to you this day my eyes, my ears, my mouth, my
heart, my whole being without reserve. Since I am
yours, my good mother, keep and guard me as your
property and possession.

Hail Mary.   [500 days, R. 340]

Prayer of Confidence in Mary

Dear Mother Mary, I come to you to place my trust
in you. I live in a world filled with temptations, a
world where it is difficult to serve you and Christ,
your Son. Despite these difficulties and my own
weakness I know that with your motherly guidance
and encouragement I can surmount the obstacles in
my path. I place all my trust in you, Mary. For you
are my mother, and always you are at my side. So
great is my love that I place myself, body and soul,
in your hands now and forever. Amen.

Immaculate Conception

You are all beautiful, O Mary, you are not stained
with original sin. ¶ You are the glory of Jerusalem,
you, the joy of Israel, you, the great honor of our
people, you, the advocate of sinners. ¶ O Mary, O
Mary, Virgin most prudent, Mother most merciful,
pray for us, intercede for us with our Lord Jesus
Christ.   [500 days, R. 359]

In Honor of the Immaculate Conception

O God, who by means of the Immaculate Conception of the Virgin prepared a worthy dwelling for Your Son and foreseeing His death preserved her from all stain; ¶ grant that we too, because of her intercession, may come to You unstained by sin, through the same Christ our Lord. Amen.

[3 years, R. 372]

Prayer in Time of Trials and Crosses

My sorrowful Mother, by the merit of that grief which you felt at seeing your beloved Jesus led to death, obtain for me the grace to bear with patience those crosses which God sends me. ¶ I will be fortunate if I also shall know how to accompany you with my cross until death. ¶ You and Jesus, both innocent, have borne a heavy cross; and shall I, a sinner, who have merited hell, refuse mine? ¶ Immaculate Virgin, I hope you will help me to bear my crosses with patience. Amen.

Saint Alphonsus Liguori

An Act of Consecration to Our Sorrowful Mother

Holy Mary, Mother of God and Queen of Martyrs, I do this day choose you as my model, protectress and advocate. ¶ In your Immaculate Heart, pierced with so many swords of sorrow, I place my poor soul forever. ¶ Receive me as your special servant, as a partaker in your sufferings. ¶ Give me strength always to remain close to that cross on which your only Son died for me. ¶ All that I am and have, I consecrate to your service. ¶ Accept every good work that I may perform and offer it to your Son for me. ¶ Dear Mother, help me to be worthy of the

68

*Add all the love children have ever had for
their mothers, mothers for their children, wives
for their husbands, saints and angels for those who
ask their help. All this love would never equal
the love Mary has for a single soul.*
Saint Alphonsus Liguori

---

title: "Servant of Mary." Stand by me in all my actions that they may be directed to the glory of God. ¶ As you were close to Christ, your Son, on the cross, be near to me, your child, in my last agony. ¶ Obtain for me, that I may invoke your and His sweet name saying with my lips and my heart: "Jesus, Mary, and Joseph, assist me in my last agony. Jesus, Mary, and Joseph, may I die in peace in your holy company." Author unknown

In Reparation for Insults to the Blessed Mother

O Blessed Virgin, Mother of God, look down in mercy from heaven where you are enthroned as Queen, upon me, a miserable sinner, your unworthy servant. ¶ Although I know full well my own unworthiness, yet in order to atone for the offenses that are done to you by impious and blasphemous tongues, from the depths of my heart I praise and proclaim you as the purest, the fairest, the holiest creature of all God's handiwork. ¶ I bless your holy name, I praise your exalted privilege of being truly Mother of God, ever virgin, conceived without stain of sin, co-redemptrix of the human race. ¶ I bless the eternal Father who chose you in a special way for His daughter; ¶ I bless the Word Incarnate who took upon Himself our nature in your bosom

69

and so made you His Mother; I bless the Holy Spirit who took you as His bride. ¶ All honor, praise, and thanksgiving to the ever-blessed Trinity who destined you and loved you so exceedingly from all eternity as to exalt you above all creatures to the most sublime heights. ¶ O Virgin, holy and merciful, obtain for all who offend you, the grace of repentance, and graciously accept this poor act of homage from me your servant, obtaining for me from your divine Son the pardon and remission of all my sins. Amen. [500 days, R. 329]

Prayer of Saint Alphonsus Liguori for Love of Mary

O Mary, you are the noblest, the most exalted, the purest, the fairest, the holiest of all things created! ¶ O that all men knew you, dearest Lady, and loved you as you deserve! ¶ But I am consoled by the thought that so many holy souls in heaven and so many just men upon the earth live enthralled by your goodness and beauty. ¶ Above all else I rejoice that God Himself loves you alone more than all men and angels. ¶ O my Queen, most worthy of love, I too love you, miserable sinner that I am, but I love you far too little; ¶ I desire a greater and more tender love of you, and this you must obtain for me; ¶ for love of you is a great sign of predestination, and a grace granted by God to those who shall be saved. ¶ Therefore, dear Mother, I see that I am under exceeding obligation to your divine Son; ¶ I see that He is deserving of infinite love. ¶ You have no other desire but to see Him loved by men; ¶ obtain for me the grace of an ardent love of Jesus Christ; ¶ win this grace for me, you who obtain from God whatever you desire. ¶ I do not seek the

things of earth, not honors, not riches; I seek only
that which your heart seeks most of all, to love God
and Him alone. ¶ Can it be that you are unwilling
to assist me in this my desire which is so dear to
you? ¶ No, you are already giving me your help;
even now you are praying for me. Pray, O Mary,
pray and never cease to pray until you shall see me
safe in paradise, where I shall be sure of possessing
and loving my God together with you, my dearest
Mother, for ever and ever. Amen.

Hail Mary (3 times). [3 years, R. 334]

Mother of Perpetual Help

O Mother of Perpetual Help, you are the dispenser
of every grace that God grants us in our misery; ¶
this is why He has made you so powerful, so rich,
so kind, that you might assist us in our miseries. ¶
You are the advocate of the most unfortunate and
abandoned sinners, if they but come to you; ¶ come
once more to my assistance, for I commend myself
to you. ¶ In your hands I place my eternal salvation; ¶ to you I entrust my soul. ¶ Enroll me among
your most faithful servants; ¶ take me under your
protection and it is enough for me; ¶ for if you protect me, I shall fear nothing; ¶ not my sins, for you
will obtain for me their pardon and remission; ¶ not
the evil spirits, for you are mightier than all the
powers of hell; ¶ not even Jesus, my judge, for He is

appeased by a single prayer from you. ¶ I fear only that through my own negligence I may forget to recommend myself to you and so I shall be lost. ¶ My dear Lady, obtain for me the forgiveness of my sins, love for Jesus, final perseverance, and the grace to have recourse to you at all times, O Mother of Perpetual Help.

Hail Mary (3 times).   [500 days, R. 427]

Queen of the Angels

Majestic Queen of heaven and Queen of the angels, you received from God the power and commission to crush the head of Satan; ¶ therefore, we humbly beseech you, send forth the legions of heaven, that under your command they may search out all evil spirits, engage them everywhere in battle, curb their insolence, and hurl them back into the pit of hell. ¶ "Who is like to God?" ¶ O good and tender Mother, you shall ever be our hope and the object of our love. ¶ O Mother of God, send forth the holy angels to defend me and drive far from me the cruel foe. Holy Angels and Archangels, defend us, keep us.

[500 days, R. 345]

The Litany of the Blessed Virgin

The term *litany* originally referred to processions of the devout held frequently in the early days of the Church. Later it applied to the responsive petition form of prayer. The "Litany of Loreto" was evolved from innumerable prayers which invoked the aid of the Blessed Virgin through addressing her by various titles. Fifty of these invocations came to be used in the diocese of Loreto and became known as the "Litany of Loreto." Twelve invocations honor Mary as the Mother of God, seven honor her virginity, and twelve her queenship. The rest are symbolic titles, inspired by various passages found in Holy Scripture.

Litany of Loreto

Lord, have mercy on us.   *Christ, have mercy on us.*
Lord, have mercy on us. Christ, hear us.
                         Christ, graciously hear us.
God the Father of heaven,   *have mercy on us.*
God the Son, Redeemer of the world,
God the Holy Spirit,
Holy Trinity, one God,

Holy Mary,   *pray for us.*
Holy Mother of God,
Holy Virgin of virgins,

Mother
     of Christ,   *pray for us.*
     of divine grace,
     most pure,
     most chaste,
     inviolate,
     undefiled,
     most amiable,
     most admirable,
     of good counsel,
     of our Creator,
     of our Savior,

Virgin most
     prudent,   *pray for us.*
     venerable,
     renowned,
     powerful,
     merciful,
     faithful,

Mirror of justice,   *pray for us.*
Seat of wisdom,
Cause of our joy,
Spiritual vessel,
Vessel of honor,
Singular vessel of devotion,
Mystical rose,
Tower of David,
Tower of ivory,
House of gold,
Ark of the Covenant,
Gate of heaven,
Morning star,
Health of the sick,
Refuge of sinners,
Comforter of the afflicted,
Help of Christians,

Queen
    of angels,   *pray for us.*
    of patriarchs,
    of prophets,
    of apostles,
    of martyrs,
    of confessors,
    of virgins,
    of all saints,
    conceived without original sin,
    assumed into heaven,
    of the most holy rosary,
    of peace,

Lamb of God, who takes away the sins of the world,
                              spare us, O Lord.
Lamb of God, who takes away the sins of the world,
                              graciously hear us, O Lord.

Lamb of God, who takes away the sins of the world,
have mercy on us.
Pray for us, O holy Mother of God,
*that we may be made worthy of the
promises of Christ.*

Let us pray. Grant, we beseech You, O Lord God,
to us Your servants, that we may rejoice in con-
tinual health of mind and body; and by the glorious
intercession of blessed Mary ever Virgin, may be
delivered from present sadness, and enter into the
joy of Your eternal gladness, through Christ our
Lord. Amen.   [7 years, R. 319]

---

*. . . you are citizens with the saints
and members of God's household.*
Ephesians 2:19

The Saints Triumphant   ☩

The world needs men of God,
men filled with sanctifying grace, the divine life,
with humility and simplicity,
with purity and penance,
with courage and joy;
men who are not for sale, but honest,
honest with their God,
honest with Mary and the saints,
honest with all their fellow men;
men not ashamed of what they profess;
men of prayer and action;
men who hope not in their own efforts, but in Me,
who pray and laugh and sorrow and love,

who fear themselves, yet trust in Me,
who, despite their weakness and nothingness,
    follow Me;
men who answer My challenge;
men of God.

Such people are the saints:
men and women who have lived and prayed and
    worked for Me,
loved and laughed and sorrowed for Me.
Saints are not wax figures,
but human beings like yourself;
speaking, thinking, feeling as you do,
willing what I will.
These are the saints—real, lovable people,
not the shadows which some make of them.

These saints are My friends.
They have given all, withholding nothing.
They have followed in My footsteps, imitating Me,
living My life on earth.
But imitating Me was not easy.
Sorrows, joys, fears, laughter, suffering, kindness—
they lived for Me.
Work, leisure, and prayer—all for Me.
It was not easy,
but it brought them happiness and peace.
Eternal happiness is theirs after a few short years,
eternal happiness with Me, My Mother, and all
    My chosen friends.

The saints are your brothers by grace;
I give them to you.
They help you
by praying for you,
by inspiring you,

by guiding you,
by living again through you.
They show you that it is possible to answer
My challenge.
With their help you can meet My challenge,
the challenge of the Christian way of life,
and in this way become a man of God—
a saint.

Devotion to Those Who Have Met the Challenge

Devotion to the saints is a life of deep and familiar companionship with them. It is more than merely saying a few prayers in their honor. It is an attitude of the mind and will that pervades one's life. You have to know someone before you can love him. We come to know the saints by reading their lives.

If we know them and love them, we will want to avoid offending them. This of course means we will avoid all kinds of deliberate sin and, conversely, will be faithful to God's will in every detail to please them.

Devotion to the saints means frequent recourse to them and remembrance of them. We will turn to them instinctively when the occasions arise. We can offer up some of our works and sufferings during the day in honor of our saint or saints.

Devotion to the saints is a trust in them, and an abandonment of ourselves to their protection. This means placing active confidence in them and living with a Christian hope and joy which realizes that nothing is too insignificant for their interest and care.

To What Saints Should We Be Devoted?

We should try to have devotion only to a few saints, but to these few we should be deeply devoted. We cannot be truly devoted to multitudes of them. These few will be determined by our particular needs, by their dignity, by our vocation, by our tastes. But in general, choose a saint or saints who particularly appeal to you.

77

Sanctity Unlimited

Sanctity is never restricted to "types" of people, because Jesus does not restrict Himself to types. He loved and loves all classes and races and types of personalities, people in every walk of life and occupation. As the cheerful brightness of a candle comes from the unity of wick, wax, and flame, so is the glory of God and the perfect personality of Christ reflected in the countless facets of human "types" in heaven. The goodness and strength and lovableness of Jesus are manifested by vari-colored rays coming from the perfect lives of His numerous canonized saints.

Prayer to One's Patron Saint

Son of Adam, son of my nature, the same by nature, differing only in grace, man, like myself, exposed to temptation, the same temptations, to the same warfare within, and without; ¶ with the same three deadly enemies—the world, the flesh, and the devil; ¶ with the same human, the same wayward heart: differing only as the power of God had changed and ruled it. ¶ You were not an Angel from Heaven but a man, whom grace, and grace alone, had made to differ from me. ¶ You preached not yourself, but Jesus Christ our Lord. My patron, Saint . . . , pray for me.   Cardinal Newman

Saint Joseph

Joseph, called in the Bible "a just man," who was never to see Jesus work a public miracle or to suffer and die, lived prayerfully and obscurely by faith; God and Mary loved him and could count on him, a hard-working, simple carpenter. He was not martyred, never preached a sermon or wrote a book, is not even mentioned in the Ordinary of the Mass; but the obedience, honesty, and hard work of this prayerful man is inspiration to millions of Catholics of all times: they, too, can count on him.

78

"There are special reasons why blessed Joseph should be explicitly named the Patron of the Church and why the Church should in turn expect much from his patronage and guardianship. For he, indeed, was the husband of Mary and the father, as was supposed, of Jesus Christ. From this arises all his dignity, grace, holiness, and glory. . . . since the bond of marriage existed between Joseph and the Blessed Virgin, there can be no doubt that more than any other person he approached that supereminent dignity by which the Mother of God is raised far above all created natures. . . . Likewise, Joseph alone stands out in august dignity because he was the guardian of the Son of God by the Divine appointment, and in the opinion of men was His father . . .

"From this double dignity, moreover, such duties arose as are prescribed by nature for the head of a household. Joseph was at once the legitimate and the natural guardian, preserver, and defender of the Divine household over which he presided. . . .

"Moreover, the Divine household, which Joseph governed as with paternal authority, contained the beginnings of the new Church. . . . Thus, it is conformable to reason, and in every way becoming to blessed Joseph, that as once it was his sacred trust to guard with watchful care the family of Nazareth, no matter what befell, so now, by virtue of his heavenly patronage, he is in turn to protect and to defend the Church of Christ."

Pope Leo XIII, *Quamquam Pluries*

An Act of Consecration to Saint Joseph

O dearest Saint Joseph, I consecrate myself to your service; I give myself to you, that you may always be my father, my protector, and my guide in the way of salvation. Obtain for me a great purity of heart, a fervent love of the interior life, and the spirit of prayer.

After your example may I do everything for the greater glory of God, in union with the divine Heart of Jesus and the Immaculate Heart of Mary. And do you, O blessed Saint Joseph, pray for me, that I may share in the peace and joy of your holy death. Amen.   Author unknown

Prayer to Saint Joseph

Saint Joseph, the "just man," the perfect man of Nazareth, the spouse of Mary, the foster father of Jesus, the patron of labor, the patron of a happy death, the patron of the whole Church, ¶ sinless, selfless, unflinchingly generous. ¶ I am a poor beggar, I am in need, my tale is against me, I am very disappointing, I have no excuse, I deserve nothing, even for the future, how much can I promise? ¶ I cannot be sure of myself, but I would it were otherwise. ¶ I would become true, and you can help me; for Jesus hears you. ¶ Ask Him to forgive, ask Him to forget, ask Him to make me sinless, like to yourself, ¶ to make me selfless, like yourself, ¶ to make me generous. ¶ Take me as your companion, and Mary's and His.   Archbishop Goodier

Worker's Prayer to Saint Joseph

Glorious Saint Joseph, pattern of all who are devoted to work, obtain for me the grace to work hard in the spirit of penance in order thereby to atone for my many sins; to labor conscientiously, putting devotion to duty before my own inclinations; to labor with thankfulness and joy, considering it an honor to employ and to develop by my labor the gifts I have received from almighty God; to work with order, peace, moderation, and patience without shrinking from weariness and difficulties; to work above all with a pure intention and with detachment from self, having always before my eyes the hour of death and the accounting which I must then render of time ill-spent, of talents unemployed, of good undone, and of my empty pride in success which is so fatal to the work of God. All for Jesus, all through Mary, all in imitation of you, O Patriarch Joseph! This shall be my motto in life and in death. Amen.

[500 days, R. 478]

Litany of Saint Joseph

Lord, have mercy on us. *Christ, have mercy on us.*
Lord, have mercy on us. Christ, hear us.

Christ, graciously hear us.

God the Father of heaven, *have mercy on us.*
God the Son, Redeemer of the world,
God the Holy Spirit,
Holy Trinity, one God,

Holy Mary, *pray for us.*
Saint Joseph,
Illustrious son of David,
Light of patriarchs,
Spouse of the Mother of God,
Chaste guardian of the Virgin,
Foster father of the Son of God,
Diligent protector of Christ,
Head of the Holy Family,

Joseph most
    just, *pray for us.*
    chaste,
    prudent,
    valiant,
    obedient,
    faithful,

Mirror of patience, *pray for us.*
Lover of poverty,
Model of laborers,
Strength of the home,
Guardian of virgins,
Safeguard of families,
Consoler of the afflicted,
Hope of the sick,
Patron of the dying,
Terror of demons,
Protector of holy Church,

Lamb of God, who takes away the sins of the world,
spare us, O Lord.
Lamb of God, who takes away the sins of the world,
graciously hear us, O Lord.
Lamb of God, who takes away the sins of the world,
have mercy on us, O Lord.
He made him lord of His house,
and prince of all His possessions.

Let us pray. O God, who in Your wondrous providence chose blessed Joseph to be the spouse of Your
most holy Mother; grant, we beseech You, that we
may deserve to have him for our intercessor in
heaven, whom on earth we venerate as our protector, who lives and reigns, world without end. Amen.
[5 years, R. 462]

Apostles

There are the tireless "apostolic" saints, such as Paul
and Francis Xavier. Their personalities and environment
were different, but the compelling motive for their ex-
haustive activity was the same: their love of and devotion
to Jesus Christ. To them life seemed too short and time
too fleeting to satisfy their driving desire to sow the
knowledge and love of their best friend in all lands. Yet

their footsteps spanned continents in the time given to them. "Saints in a hurry" they have been called, but our Lord is not restricted to this type of individual. We see a gracious Claude de la Colombiere who was chosen by God to bring the message of the Sacred Heart to all men. There is Martin de Porres, the kind American Negro, patron of social justice, whose gentle and determined love of God led him to sacrifice himself for his fellow men. There are the apostles who never leave the monastery or cloister, but who, by their prayers and sacrifices, bring down God's grace to the human race. Such was Saint Thérèse of Lisieux, named co-patron with Xavier of those who labor in the foreign missions. All apostles, though they differ widely in time, in state of life and talents, have two things in common: a strong, driving love for Jesus Christ and a ceaseless zeal for souls. For them nothing is too dangerous or foolish or difficult. For love counts no cost.

Prayer to Saint Peter, Prince of the Apostles

O glorious Saint Peter, as a reward for your lively and generous faith, your profound and sincere humility, and your ardent love, you were singled out by our Lord and endowed with most special privileges. You were also constituted prince of the apostles, with primacy over the whole Church, of which you were made the rock and foundation. Obtain for us, we pray, a lively faith and an ardent zeal so that all of us will labor for the return of our separated brothers. May the desire of our divine Redeemer, that there might be but "one Fold and one Shepherd," be for us, as it was for you, the inspiration to work and pray for the return of all those who are still outside the Fold. Strengthened by divine grace, may they be led back speedily to the bosom of our common mother, the Catholic Church. Amen.

Author unknown

Prayer to Saint Paul

O glorious Saint Paul, from a persecutor of the Christian name you became an apostle of burning zeal, and in order that Jesus Christ might become known to the furthermost bounds of the earth, you joyfully suffered imprisonment, scourging, stoning, shipwreck, and every kind of persecution. Obtain for us now the grace to pray at all times for those who have not as yet been blessed with the gift of faith. Help us to use all our strength for the conversion of those who have not as yet heard the name of our Lord and Savior, Jesus Christ. Amen.

O Lord, grant me Saint Paul's love; a love fervent, eager, energetic, active, full of great work, "strong as death," a flame which "many waters could not quench, nor the streams drown," which lasted to the end, when he could say: "I have fought the good fight, I have finished my course, I have kept the faith. As to the rest, there is laid up for me a crown of justice, which the Lord the just judge will render to me in that day." Amen.   Author unknown

Novena of Grace

The devotion in honor of Saint Francis Xavier, now called the Novena of Grace, owes its origin to the saint himself. In 1633 the saint appeared to a dying Jesuit priest, asked the father to repeat his promise to go to the Indian Missions, and then cured him. During this same apparition Xavier also assured the Jesuit that all who would call on him for nine days would receive whatever they asked if what they wanted would contribute to their eternal salvation.

O most lovable and loving Saint Francis Xavier, in union with you I reverently adore the divine majesty. While joyfully giving thanks to God for the singular

84

gifts of grace bestowed upon you during your life and your gifts of glory after death, I beseech you with all my heart's devotion to be pleased to obtain for me, by your efficacious intercession, the greatest of all blessings: the grace of living a holy life and dying a holy death. Moreover, I beg of you to obtain for me *(here mention the favor you desire)*. But if what I ask of you so earnestly does not tend to the glory of God and the good of my soul, obtain for me, I pray, what is more conducive to both. Amen.

Our Father, Hail Mary, Glory be.

[3 years, R. 500]

Prayer in Honor of the Little Flower, Co-Patron of the Missions

O God, who inflamed with Your spirit of love the soul of Saint Thérèse of the Child Jesus, grant that we too may love You and make You loved exceedingly. Amen.   [300 days, R. 577]

Martyrs

The Holy Innocents were the first Christian martyrs, the first to shed their blood in witness to Christ. After them has come the endless procession of men and women, girls and boys, who have preferred to die rather than deny their faith. Martyrs are gaunt and resolute men of prayer and penance like John the Baptist. But they are also frail young women like Lucy or Agnes or Cecilia, who were strong in their faith and the desire to die before betraying the promise of their virginity. Martyrdom is no respecter of persons. Thomas More, author and statesman under Henry VIII, won his martyr's crown because he was more loyal to the King of heaven than to a king of this earth. Many are the missionaries like Isaac Jogues and John de Brebeuf who suffered torture and death at the hands of those they came to save. Maria Goretti died rather than commit a sin of impurity. Many other Christians have died nameless during every period of history in cruel and often prolonged bloody purges. In recent years a countless number of Christians have been called upon—in Mexico, in Spain, in Nazi Germany, and now behind the Iron Curtain—to bear witness to Christ with their blood. They stand with the Queen of Martyrs beneath the cross of Christ. They are "filling up," to use the words of Saint Paul, "what is wanting to the sufferings of Christ." They are continuing Calvary on earth. Down through the ages and right up to the present day, echoes the cry of the early Christian persecutor, Julian the Apostate, who seeing the bravery and loyalty of these friends of Christ exclaimed, "Thou hast conquered, O Galilean!"

Prayer to Saint John the Baptist

O martyr invincible, who, for the honor of God and the salvation of souls, withstood with firmness and constancy the impiety of Herod even at the cost of your own life, and rebuked him openly for his wicked and dissolute life; ¶ by your prayers obtain for us a heart brave and generous, in order that we may overcome all human respect and openly profess our faith in loyal obedience to the teachings of Jesus Christ, our divine Master.   [R. 457]

Prayer to Saint Tarcisius

Teach us, Saint Tarcisius, to love and appreciate the most Holy Sacrament, the body and blood, soul and divinity, of our Lord Jesus Christ. ¶ You died willingly rather than give into the hands of unbelievers the Bread of Life. ¶ Inspire us with your faith. ¶ Make our charity strong and manly as was yours and obtain for us the gift of hope that we may one day enjoy with you the reward promised by Jesus Christ: "He who eats My flesh and drinks My blood has life everlasting."

Prayer to Saint Agnes, Virgin and Martyr

A singular example of virtue, glorious Saint Agnes, by the living faith which animated you from your tenderest years and rendered you so pleasing to God that you merited the martyr's crown, obtain for us the grace to keep our holy faith inviolate within us and to profess ourselves Christians sincerely in word and work. ¶ May our open confession of Jesus before men cause Him to bear a favorable witness to us before His eternal Father.

Our Father, Hail Mary, Glory be.

[300 days, R. 560]

Prayer to Saint Thomas More

By your death, Saint Thomas More, you proclaimed your loyalty to Christ the King. ¶ Teach us to value our faith above all the honors of this world and to treasure it above all the joys of earth. ¶ Despite the fears that beset you, you remained calm and cheerful to the end. ¶ Obtain for us the grace to bear cheerfully the little martyrdoms of our daily life so that if the time should ever come when we are asked to proclaim our loyalty with our lives, we may die as you did with a smile on our lips and the love of God in our heart. Amen.

Prayer from the Mass of the North American Martyrs

O God, who has hallowed the first fruits of the faith in the northern regions of America by the preaching and blood of Your blessed martyrs, John, Isaac, and their companions, grant in Your mercy, that through their intercession, the plentiful harvest of the faithful may increase everywhere from day to day, through Christ our Lord. Amen.   Lefebvre

Prayer to Saint Maria Goretti

Saint Maria Goretti, by your prayers gain for me the courage to be a chaste and loyal friend of Jesus Christ. ¶ Help me always to be proud of His friendship and to value it highly. ¶ Protect me from the confusing whispers of temptation. ¶ Help me to remember, when it is so easy to forget, how much Christ really means to me. ¶ Teach me to respect the people I love so that our love may be lasting and good and pleasing to God. Amen.

Confessors

Not all the saints were called upon to shed their blood for Christ. God's plan for them was otherwise. Augustine was not called upon to shed his blood in witness to Christ. Instead, by the holiness of his life and the power of his writings, this former sinner and man of the world bore witness to Christ and continues to do so in every age. So do all the confessors among God's saints. Some were converts from a life of sin: women like Mary Magdalene or Margaret of Cortona, men like Camillus de Lellis, founder of the Red Cross. Others were writers and teachers like Thomas Aquinas and Francis de Sales, or souls devoted to the contemplation of God, like Teresa of Avila and John of the Cross. The founders of religious orders, Francis, Ignatius, Dominic, Madeleine Sophie Barat, and countless others, not only confessed Christ through their own lives, but left behind them a spiritual family to continue the spirit of love and devotion which had characterized their lives. Philip Neri, a jovial saint of the "personal appeal," used his one great talent, a pleasant personality, to win souls to Christ. Margaret Mary, a humble nun of Paray-le-Monial, became the recipient of the tremendous revelations of the love of the Sacred Heart for men. Missionaries like Xavier and those to whom they brought the faith like Kateri Tekakwitha combined in their lives the confession of Christ in all lands and tongues. The Curé d'Ars, John Vianney, brought Christ to a fallen-away parish in the country-side of France; Frances Cabrini hurried halfway around the earth to confess His name among the emigrants to the New World; Pope Pius X showed his great love by bringing the Eucharist within the reach of all. Men and women, laymen and popes, priests and nuns, the great army of the Church Militant, these are the confessors of Christ. Different as may be their roles in the kingdom of Christ they all unite in their great personal love of Jesus Christ and their zeal to bring His message to all men. Jesus of Nazareth still walks the earth through His friends, His saints.

Prayer to Saint Anne, Mother of the Blessed Virgin

With a heart full of the most sincere reverence I kneel before you, singularly privileged and glorious Saint Anne. ¶ Through your outstanding virtues and holiness you merited from God the high favor of giving life to her who is the treasury of all graces, the blessed among women, mother of the Word made flesh, the most holy Virgin Mary. ¶ May I be received, most understanding saint, into the number of your devoted servants, for so I profess myself and so I wish to remain for the rest of my life. ¶ Shield me with your unfailing patronage and obtain for me from God the ability to imitate those virtues which were your own in such abundance. ¶ Let me know my sins and be heartily sorry for them. ¶ Obtain for me the grace of an eager love for Jesus and Mary and the resoluteness I need to fulfill the obligations of my calling faithfully and constantly. ¶ Save me from these dangers which are and will be mine in life ¶ and help me in the hour of my death so that I may at last arrive safely in paradise to sing with you, happiest of mothers, the praises of the Word of

God become man within your most pure daughter, the Virgin Mary.

Our Father, Hail Mary, Glory be (3 times).

[300 days, R. 494]

Prayer in Honor of Saint Dominic

Merciful Redeemer, You selected Saint Dominic to toil with You in saving souls; and he in turn, by his eagerness and the help of Your grace, won over in great numbers heretics once cut off from the Church and sinners who had saddened the Church by their scandalous lives. Now, my God, send more and more fresh laborers into Your vineyard to toil for Your glory and afterwards to reap the harvest of the everlasting life.

Prayer in Honor of Saint Ignatius Loyola

O God, who for the spreading of the greater glory of Your name, by means of blessed Ignatius strengthened the Church Militant with a new army, grant that by his aid and by his example we may so fight on earth as to become worthy to be crowned with him in heaven, through Christ our Lord. Amen.

Lefebvre

Prayer to Saint Anthony of Padua

O wondrous Saint Anthony, glorious and famed for your miracles, you had the happiness of receiving in your arms our Blessed Lord, disguised as a small child. ¶ From His goodness obtain for me this favor which I desire with all my heart . . .

You were so gracious to poor sinners. ¶ Do not look then upon the unworthiness of him who calls on you but upon the glory of God which, through you, will be exalted once again through the salvation of my soul and through the granting of my earnest request.

As a sign of my gratitude I beg you to accept my promise to live from now on more perfectly in accord with the teachings of the Gospel and to be devoted to the service of the poor whom you loved and still love so much. ¶ Bless my resolution and obtain for me the grace to be faithful to it even until death. Amen.   [300 days, R. 532]

Prayer to Saint Paul of the Cross
O glorious Saint Paul of the Cross, who, by meditating on the Passion of Jesus Christ, attained so high a degree of holiness on earth and of happiness in heaven. By preaching the same Passion you offered anew to the world the most certain cure for all its ills. Win for us the grace to keep the Passion ever deeply engraved in our hearts, that so we may be able to reap the same fruits both in time and in eternity. Amen.

Our Father, Hail Mary, Glory be.
[300 days, R. 510]

Prayer in Honor of Saint Margaret Mary
O Lord Jesus Christ who did in a wondrous manner reveal to the blessed virgin Margaret the unsearchable riches of Your Heart; grant us, through her merits and example, that we may love You in all things and above all things, and become worthy to dwell within Your Heart for evermore, who lives and reigns, God, world without end. Amen.

Lefebvre

Prayer to Saint Vincent de Paul
Glorious Saint Vincent, heavenly patron of all charitable societies, and father of all the poor, while you were on earth you never turned away any one who

came to you. ¶ Consider the evils that oppress us and come to our assistance. ¶ Obtain from your Lord help for the poor, ¶ relief for the infirm, ¶ consolation for the afflicted, ¶ protection for the abandoned, ¶ a spirit of generosity for the rich, ¶ the grace of conversion for sinners, ¶ zeal for priests, ¶ peace for the Church, ¶ tranquillity and order for all nations ¶ and salvation for them all. Let all men prove the effects of your merciful intercession so that, being helped by you in the miseries of this life, we may be united to you in the life to come where there shall be no more grief, nor weeping, nor sorrow but joy and gladness and everlasting happiness. Amen.   [300 days, R. 513]

Prayer to Saint Thérèse of the Child Jesus

O marvelous Saint Thérèse of the Child Jesus, who, in your brief mortal career, became a mirror of angelic purity, of daring love, and of wholehearted surrender to almighty God, now that you are enjoying the reward of your virtues, turn your eyes of mercy upon us who trust in you. Win for us the grace to keep our hearts and minds pure and clean as yours and to abhor in all sincerity whatever might tarnish ever so slightly the luster of a virtue so sublime, a virtue that endears us to your heavenly bridegroom. Dear saint, grant us to feel in every need the power of your intercession; give us comfort in all the bitterness of this life, and especially at its end, that we may be worthy to share eternal happiness with you in paradise. Amen.

Pray for us, O blessed Thérèse,
that we may be made worthy of the
promises of Christ.

Let us pray. O Lord, who said: "Unless you become as little children, you shall not enter into the kingdom of heaven"; grant us, we beseech You, so to walk in the footsteps of Your blessed virgin Thérèse with a humble and single heart, that we may attain to everlasting rewards: who lives and reigns world without end. Amen. [300 days, R. 576]

Prayer to Saint Aloysius, Patron of Youth

Saint Aloysius, youth of angelic life, I, your unworthy supplicant, recommend especially to you the chastity of my soul and body, praying you, by your angelic purity, to plead for me with Jesus Christ, the immaculate Lamb, and His most holy Mother, the Virgin of virgins, and to keep me from all grievous sin. ¶ Never let me stain my soul with any impurity, but when you see me in temptation or in danger of sinning, put far from my heart all unclean thoughts and affections, awakening in me the memory of eternity and of Jesus crucified. ¶ Impress deeply in my heart a sense of the holy fear of God. ¶ Enkindle in me the fire of divine love and obtain for me so to follow your footsteps here on earth that I may merit to enjoy with you in heaven the vision of our God forever. Amen. [R. 496]

Prayer to Saint John Berchmans, Patron of Those Who Serve Mass

Saint John, young and pure of heart, but full of manly virtue, you were a stalwart soldier in the Company of Jesus and an ardent defender of the Immaculate Conception of the Blessed Virgin Mary. The all-wise providence of God has set you forth as a shining example to reveal the treasures of holiness which result from the devoted and holy fulfillment of the common duties of life. I earnestly beg you to make me ever constant and faithful in observing the duties of my state in life. Make me pure of heart, fearless and strong against the enemies of my eternal salvation, and cheerfully obedient to the promptings of God's holy will. By your singular devotion to the loving Mother of Jesus, who looked upon you as her own dear son, obtain for me the grace of a fervent love for Jesus and Mary and the power of drawing others to this love. Amen.   [R. 527]

I am the resurrection and the life;
he who believes in me, even if he die, shall live.
John 11:25

The Saints Suffering

Some of My friends suffer in purgatory.
They died in the state of grace,
but must endure terrible pains
to purify and cleanse them
in expiation for past sin
so that they may enter heaven and see God.
I ask you to help these holy souls:
pray for them;
gain indulgences for them;
offer your works and sufferings for them.
They need your help,
for they cannot help themselves.
They will be eternally grateful to you
and will beg from Me special graces for you.
Remember: whatever you do for one of these
you do for Me.

94

De Profundis, Psalm 129

Out of the depths I cry to you, O Lord; O Lord hear my voice!

Let your ears be attentive to the voice of my supplication.

If you should remember sins, O Lord; O Lord, who could bear it?

But with you is forgiveness, that you may be served with reverence.

I hope in the Lord, my soul hopes in his word;

My soul waits for the Lord, more than watchmen for the dawn.

More than watchmen for the dawn, let Israel wait for the Lord,

For with the Lord is mercy and with him plenteous redemption:

And he shall redeem Israel from all its sins.

Eternal rest give to them, O Lord. And let perpetual light shine upon them. May they rest in peace. Amen. O Lord, hear my prayer. And let my cry come to you.

Let us pray. O God, the Creator and Redeemer of all the faithful, grant to the souls of Your servants departed the remission of all their sins, that through pious supplications they may obtain the pardon which they have always desired, who lives and reigns, world without end. Amen.

May they rest in peace. Amen.

[3 years, R. 585]

Offering of Masses for the Dying

My God, I offer You all the Masses which are being celebrated today throughout the whole world, for sinners who are in their agony and who are to die this day. ¶ May the precious blood of Jesus, their Redeemer, obtain mercy for them.   Rickaby

For Priests

O God, who in the ranks of the apostolic priesthood invested these, Your servants, with the pontifical or priestly dignity, grant, we beg You, that they may be joined to the everlasting friendship of the same priests, through Christ our Lord. Amen.

[3 years, R. 599]

For Parents

O God, who commanded us to honor our father and our mother, in Your mercy have pity on the souls of my father and mother, and forgive them their trespasses and make me to see them again in the joy of everlasting brightness, through Christ our Lord. Amen.   [3 years, R. 598]

For the Faithful Departed

My Jesus, by the sorrows You suffered in Your agony in the garden, in Your scourging and crowning with thorns, in the way to Calvary, in Your crucifixion and death, have mercy on the souls in purgatory, and especially on those that are most forsaken. ¶ Deliver them from the dire torments they endure. ¶ Call them and admit them ¶ to Your most sweet embrace in paradise.

Our Father, Hail Mary, Eternal rest . . .

[500 days, R. 596]

The Saints Militant

Through baptism you received sanctifying grace,
through baptism you were admitted into My Church.
You became a member of My mystical body
and were associated with all the other members.

The stranger at the altar rail,
the priest in the pulpit,
the missionary on the other side of the world—
you and they are all members of one body;
you and they all share the divine life through grace.
As members of the same living body you need
one another
just as the hand needs the arm,
just as the arm needs the head.
The whole body must work harmoniously
to accomplish My work upon earth.
Each member is united to every other;
each member should help every other;
each member must strive to keep himself holy
and thus win grace and strength for the whole body.

It is part of My challenge that you pray and work
for the well-being of My mystical body
throughout the world:
that the members who are spiritually sick
become well,
that all men join themselves to the body.

First of all you must pray and work
for your own spiritual health,
for your own perfection.
Then you must pray and work
for your family,
for your friends,
for your parish,
for your diocese.
Finally, you must pray and work
for all the members throughout the world;
you must pray and work
for the triumph of My kingdom upon earth.

An Act of Dedication of the Human Race

Most sweet Jesus, Redeemer of the human race, look
down upon us humbly prostrate in Your presence
(*in a church say*: before Your altar). We are Yours,
and Yours we wish to be; but to be more surely
united to You, behold, each one of us this day freely
dedicates himself to Your most Sacred Heart. Many,
indeed, have never known You; many, too, despising
Your precepts, have rejected You. Have mercy on
them all, most merciful Jesus, and draw them to
Your Sacred Heart. May You be King, O Lord, not
only of the faithful who have never forsaken You,
but also of the prodigal sons who have abandoned
You; grant that they may quickly return to their
Father's house, lest they perish of wretchedness and
hunger. May You be King of those whom heresy
holds in error or discord keeps aloof; call them back
to the harbor of truth and the unity of faith, so that
soon there may be but one fold and one shepherd.
May You be King of all those who even now sit in
the shadow of idolatry of Islam, and refuse not to
bring them into the light of Your kingdom. Look,
finally, with eyes of pity upon the children of that

race, which was for so long a time Your chosen people; and let Your blood, which was once invoked upon them in vengeance, now descend upon them also in a cleansing flood of redemption and eternal life.

Grant, O Lord, to Your Church assurance of freedom and immunity from harm; to all nations give an ordered tranquillity; bring it to pass that from pole to pole the earth may resound with one cry: Praise to the divine Heart that wrought our salvation; to it be honor and glory for ever and ever. Amen.   [5 years, R. 271]

A Morning Prayer

Lord God almighty, who has safely brought us to the beginning of this day, defend us in the same by Your mighty power, that this day we may fall into no sin, but that all our words may so proceed, and all our thoughts and actions may be so directed as to do always that which is just in Your sight, through Christ our Lord. Amen.   [5 years, R. 60]

Saint Edmund's Prayer

Into Your hands, O Lord, and into the hands of Your holy angels, I commit and entrust this day my soul, my relations, my benefactors, my friends and enemies, and all Your Catholic people. Keep us, O Lord, through the day, by the merits and intercession of the Blessed Virgin Mary and of all Your saints, from all vicious and unruly desires, from all sins and temptations of the devil, and from sudden and unprovided death and the pains of hell. Illuminate my heart with the grace of Your Holy Spirit; grant that I may ever be obedient to Your commandments; suffer me not to be separated from You,

O God, who lives and reigns with God the Father and the same Holy Spirit for ever and ever. Amen.

[3 years, R. 55]

Prayer for Peace in Our Times

Give peace in our times, O Lord, because there is none other that fights for us, but only You, O our God.

Peace be within your walls.
And abundance within your towers.

Let us pray. O God, from whom all holy desires, all right counsels and all just works do proceed; give to Your servants that peace which the world cannot give, that both our hearts may be set to obey Your commandments, and also that we, being delivered from the fear of our enemies, may pass our time, under Your protection, in rest and quietness, through Christ our Lord. Amen.   [3 years, R. 701]

Prayer for Peace

Lord Jesus Christ, who said to Your apostles: "Peace I leave with you, My peace I give to you; not as the world gives, do I give to you," regard not our sins, but Your merits, ¶ and grant to all Your servants that they whom the almighty Father has created and governs and whom You have redeemed with Your precious blood and have ordained for life everlasting, may love one another with all their hearts for Your sake and may be made one in spirit and rejoice in Your perpetual peace. ¶ Lord Jesus Christ, concerning whom the prophet has said: "And all kings of the earth shall adore Him, all nations shall serve Him," extend Your reign over the whole human race. ¶ Send upon all men the light of Your faith, deliver them from all the snares and bonds of passion, and direct them to heavenly things. ¶ And graciously grant that the states and nations may be united by means of Your immaculate bride, holy Church, and, through the intercession of the Blessed Virgin Mary, queen of peace, may serve You in all humility; ¶ and that all tongues and peoples may form one great choir to praise You both day and night, to bless You, to exalt You, O King and ruler of nations, O Prince of Peace, immortal King of ages. Amen.

[500 days, R. 703]

A Prayer for the Pope

Lord Jesus, protect our holy father . . . , from all harm. It was You who told the first pope, Saint Peter, "On this rock I will build My Church, and the gates of hell shall not prevail against it." When the powers of evil are marshaled against Your Church, give its leader the guidance and strength of Your grace. Enlighten his mind to govern the Church in accord with Your will. Keep him strong in body and soul. Give to the Church under his care victory over the hearts of men, so that all may be one with You. Amen.

Prayer for Our Nation

Smile down upon our country, Mary, for we have chosen you, immaculate Mother, our special patron and advocate. Show us, then, your love and your solicitude. Beg your Son to bless our nation's leaders —the president, the Congress, the courts. Ask Him to enlighten them to govern wisely, to protect the interests of all citizens with justice and true charity, and to respect and love His law.

But most of all, dear Mother, ask your divine Son to give all Americans the gift of the true faith. Ask Him to fire our hearts with the desire to spread His spirit and life in the hearts of our fellow countrymen so that His charity will overflow the land. Finally, Mary, inspire us with a true patriotism for this earthly home and then, after a life of faithful service to Jesus and to our country, may we come as a nation safely back to our true home, to you and to Jesus. Amen.

A Consecration for Families

O Jesus, our most loving Redeemer, who having come to enlighten the world with Your teaching and example, wished to pass the greater part of Your life in humility and subjection to Mary and Joseph in the poor home of Nazareth, thus sanctifying the family that was to be an example for all Christian families, graciously receive our family as it dedicates and consecrates itself to You this day. ¶ Defend us, guard us, and establish among us your holy fear, true peace and concord in Christian love; ¶ in order that by conforming ourselves to the divine pattern of Your family we may be able, all of us without exception, to attain to eternal happiness. ¶ Mary, dear Mother of Jesus and our mother, by your kindly intercession make this our humble offering acceptable in the sight of Jesus and obtain for us His graces and blessings.

O Saint Joseph, most holy guardian of Jesus and Mary, assist us by your prayers in all our spiritual and temporal necessities; so that we may be enabled to praise our divine Savior Jesus, together with Mary and you, for all eternity. Amen.

Our Father, Hail Mary, Glory be (3 times).

[500 days, R. 706]

For Parents

O God, whom we obey in honoring our parents, look down mercifully, I beseech You, on those to whom in Your providence I owe my being. ¶ May they grow daily in faith, hope, and charity. ¶ Implant deeply in their hearts the conviction that as You are the beginning of all things so to You must all return. ¶ Condone their frailties, pardon whatever excessive indulgence for me they may have shown and impute not to them my waywardness, my sloth, my weakness of will. ¶ Grant them while life lasts health and prosperity, pour upon them the abundance of Your grace. ¶ Defend and preserve them by Your all-powerful hand. ¶ May my Christian life, in meeting their fondest expectations and fulfilling all their hopes, be the consolation of their last years. ¶ May they die the death of the just. ¶ May they pass quickly to their heavenly home, and may I join them there, their dutiful child for all eternity. Amen.

Daniel Lord

Prayer for My Father

I thank You, dear God, for giving me my father. Enlighten me, so I may realize the depth of his love for me and the greatness of his sacrifices for me. His fatherly care reflects Your goodness; his manliness, Your strength; his understanding, Your wisdom. He is Your faithful servant and image. Bless him with peace of soul, health of body, and success in his work. Amen.

Prayer for My Mother

Lord Jesus, look with mercy and love upon my mother. Reward her untiring generosity, her love, her care of me. I ask for her the same blessings You desired for Your Mother: health of body, peace of soul, happiness of family, and the bountiful grace of God. Give her the richest joy of a mother's heart, that her child may grow in wisdom and grace before God and men. Amen.

A Prayer for Children

O my Jesus, friend of little children, You who from Your youth grew in wisdom and grace before God and men, who, the God of Your parents, subjected Yourself to them in everything, watch with special care, we beg You, these children whom we have helped You create. ¶ Help them control the new powers which will come to them; ¶ their understanding that they may clearly know Your will; ¶ their will, that they may courageously follow it. ¶ Grant that they may grow in wisdom, understanding the world, its tricks and deceits, its beauty and its transience, finally desiring, as You did, nothing but the will of Your and their Father. ¶ Above all, O most gentle Savior, let them grow in grace, never for a minute of their lives living in the darkness of sin outside of the warmth and light of Your friendship. ¶ O Christ, who grew as any other child, You know the trials and terrors they face; ¶ fill their minds with knowledge, fill their hearts with courage, fill their lives with Your love. Amen.

Prayer for Family

May Your presence, most Sacred Heart of Jesus, ever bless our home and fill it with the virtues so perfectly practiced in Your own Holy Family at Nazareth. Protect us from all dangers, bless our endeavors, and keep always in our family the spirit of love, peace, and happiness. Amen.

104

For Those I Do Not Like or Have Harmed

In the perfect prayer, merciful Jesus, You taught us to pray: "Forgive us our debts as we forgive our debtors." I am deep in Your debt, yet again and again You forgive me. How can I be other than forgiving when I see Your mercy to sinners and when—even more amazing—I have known times without number Your mercy and forgiveness. I nailed You to the cross. I have spoiled Your work, affronted You with apathy and ingratitude. Yet You forgive me again and again, take me back into Your love. How can I dislike anyone when You are merciful to everyone? Bless those for whom I feel dislike, resentment, or the desire for revenge. Where I have done anything wrong, undo the harm by Your grace, and by another miracle of mercy, give me the grace at least to like those whom I now find difficult or unattractive. Give me some of Your universal love. Amen.

Daniel Lord

Prayer before a Date

Be with us, Mother Mary, on our date this evening, so that you may share with us the enjoyment of our companionship and may keep us safe from all harm to our bodies and our souls. May the shining ideal of your purity guide us in all that we do so that our whole evening together may be for the praise and glory of your divine Son. Amen.

Prayer of an Athlete

O God, we thank You for our strong and agile bodies and for the fight and determination that gives spirit to our games. Help us to win when Your wisdom and providence desire it, but teach us also to accept our defeats without despair, since they too are willed by You. Give us the grace always to use the powers of our bodies for the victory of our souls, and to refer all praise of ourselves to Your greater honor and glory. Amen.

Prayer to Mary for Studies

Under your patronage, dear Mother, and invoking the mystery of your Immaculate Conception, I desire to pursue my studies and my literary labors. I hereby solemnly declare that I am devoting myself to these studies chiefly to the following end: that I may the better contribute to the glory of God and to the spread of your veneration among men. I pray you, therefore, most loving Mother, who are the seat of wisdom, to bless my labors in your loving kindness. Moreover, I promise with true affection and a willing spirit, as it is right that I should do so, to ascribe all the good that shall accrue to me therefrom, wholly to your intercession for me in God's holy presence. Amen.   [300 days, R. 763]

Prayer for Success in Study

Give me, Lord, a mind that learns when it is taught. Help me use my intellect for something bigger and better than myself alone. Make me want knowledge that I may know You better, so that I can love and defend Your Church, so that I can become a complete, fully developed, human being.

Let me carry my knowledge humbly. Make me realize it is a gift from God and must be returned to God.

Send Your Holy Spirit to help me see clearly, to judge wisely, to love what is true, to direct my mind to all that is good and noble and beautiful in heaven and earth.

Use me as Your special instrument, an intelligent instrument, in spreading Your kingdom throughout the whole world until all the world knows You as I know You, and knowing You, loves You. Amen.

Prayer of the Worker

Lord Jesus, carpenter of Nazareth, You were a worker as I am. Give to me and all the workers of the world the privilege to work as You did so that everything we do may be to the benefit of our fellow men and the greater glory of God the Father. May Your kingdom come into the factories and into the shops, into our homes and into our streets. Give us this day our daily bread. May we receive it without envy or injustice. To us who labor and are heavily burdened send speedily the refreshment of Your love. May we never sin against You. Show us Your way to work, and when it is done, may we with all our fellow workers rest in peace. Amen.

In Sickness and Pain

Lord, Your will be done; I take this for my sins. I offer up to You my sufferings, together with all that my Savior has suffered for me; and I beg of You, through His sufferings, to have mercy on me.

Free me from this illness and pain if You will, and if it be for my good. You love me too much to let me suffer unless it be for my good. Therefore, O Lord, I trust myself to You; do with me as You please. In sickness and in health, I wish to love You always. Amen.

A Night Prayer of Saint Alphonsus Liguori

Jesus Christ my God, I adore You and thank You for all the graces You have given me this day. I offer

You my sleep and all the moments of this night, and I beseech You to keep me without sin. Wherefore I put myself within Your sacred side and under the mantle of our Lady, my mother. Let Your holy angels stand about me and keep me in peace, and let Your blessings be upon me. Amen.

[3 years, R. 99]

A Prayer for Salvation

Help us, O God, our Savior, and for the glory of Your name deliver us and forgive us our sins for Your name's sake.

For the glory of Your name, deliver us.
And forgive us our sins for Your name's sake.

Let us pray. Mercifully hear the prayers of Your people, we beseech You, O Lord, that we who are justly afflicted for our sins, may be mercifully delivered from the same for the glory of Your holy name, through Christ our Lord. Amen.   [3 years, R. 726]

Psalm 53

O God, save me by your name, and defend my cause by your might.

O God, hear my prayer; give heed to the words of my mouth.

For proud men have risen against me, and violent men have sought my life; they have not set God before them.

Behold, God helps me, the Lord is the support of my life.

Make the evil recoil upon my enemies and according to your faithfulness destroy them.

Gladly will I sacrifice to you, I will praise your name, O Lord, for it is good.

For he has delivered me from all adversity, and my eye has seen my enemies put to shame.

. . . sin shall not have dominion over you.
Romans 6:14

Daily Examination of Conscience ☩

I challenged you to do great things for God,
to fight under the standard of our Mother,
to seek the greater glory of God.
I challenged you to live the life of grace.
Your generous soul responded to My challenge.
You offered yourself for My service.
But I do not call you servant,
I call you friend.
For you are My Mother's child;
you are a child of God.
My Sacred Heart and the Immaculate Heart of
    My Mother
desire a close friendship with you.
We offer you our hearts.
But friendship asks for a return—
you must give us your heart.
I know that you want to be our friend,
that you want to be generous,
that you want to offer us a noble, pure heart.
I know how hard it is to keep your heart
from growing hard amid the selfishness of the world,

from growing cold amid the evils of the world,
from growing false amid the deceits of the world.
And so I offer you a plan, a strategy, a practice
which will help you to purify your heart,
to make it strong, courageous, and unselfish,
to make it grace-filled,
the heart of a loyal friend.

The plan I offer you is simple but necessary;
it is a proof of loyalty;
it is called the examination of conscience.
The examen is a most excellent way to preserve the
    life of grace.
The saints have made use of the examen
to mount to great heights of love for Me.
Every night Catholics all over the world
pause and examine their souls in My presence.
My Mother expects to see you raise your mind to
God every evening
to see you review the past day,
to hear you thank God and her for the day's gifts,
to hear you humbly acknowledge your failings,
to hear you beg pardon and resolve to do better.
Our Blessed Mother wants you to be faithful to the
    examen.
I know that you will not disappoint her,
that you will be eager to use this necessary practice,
that you will purify your heart,
make it more receptive to grace,
and offer and unite it to Mine.
I know you will persevere in your nightly examen.
For you are My friend.

What Is the Examen?

"Put on the Lord Jesus Christ." The daily examination of conscience is aimed at helping us "put on Christ" in every thought, word, and action of the day. Mental prayer gives us the mind of Christ; the examination of conscience is a checkup to see how we are living out our inspirations from prayer.

We try to please those we love, a love shown in deeds, not merely in words. The examen makes our love of God practical. It indicates our loyalty in imitating Christ.

At the end of each flight the fighter pilot hands his plane over to the ground crew who check every inch of it for weakened parts, deterioration, and needed repairs. They ready it for tomorrow's flight. That is what the examen does for our soul. It reveals our weak spots— our sins; it shows us where we are deteriorating with the rust of bad habits. By sincere contrition and firm resolution the damage is repaired, and we are ready for another effort to soar higher in the service and love of our Lord.

How Is It Made?

There is no ironclad method. It is a review of the past day accompanied by contrition and a resolution to do better. As long as these essentials are covered the soul is free to speak to God in whatever words it chooses. We may use any method we find helpful, always with the approval of our spiritual director.

One of the best and most popular methods is that of Saint Ignatius. It comprises five points:

Gratitude: After putting ourselves in the presence of God, we look at the blessings with which God has enriched this day, and thank Him for them. The examen is a positive prayer. By considering God's personal gifts to us, our hearts are expanded with loving gratitude.

Petition for light: We ask God's help to see ourselves as we are, as He sees us. Without God's help we can easily be fooled by ourselves or by the devil.

Review of the day: We try to realize God's goodness to us, to recognize our successes and failures. We want to know not only how, but why we have sinned or been unfaithful to God. With such knowledge we may plan carefully to avoid that pitfall tomorrow. The day can be reviewed according to time—morning, afternoon, and evening—or according to our thoughts, words, and actions.

Contrition: Considering our ingratitude in the face of God's gifts, the suffering of our Lord in the Passion, His agony on the cross—we make a fervent act of perfect contrition. Our Lord is so anxious to be merciful; there is nothing He will not forgive.

Resolution: Having seen where, when, and why we have fallen short of our ideal of love and service of our Lord, we calmly and quietly tell Him that we will try to do better tomorrow. With the aid of His grace and light, we devise a practical plan for improving. We must not be discouraged by the frequency of our failures; we do not become saints overnight. The only real failure is to become discouraged.

When, Where, How Long?

The best time for the examination of conscience is in the evening just before retiring. Actually the examen is a natural part of night prayers; many people make an examination of conscience each night and are not aware of it. What could be more natural than to pause at the end of a day, thank God for His blessings, tell Him we are sorry for our sins and poor conduct, and resolve to make tomorrow better? It is a natural prayer.

The usual place to make our examen is in the privacy of our room, but this may not always be possible. As long as there is sufficient peace and quiet to collect one's thoughts and raise the mind to God, any place will do for the examen.

The length of the examen has no set limit, but in general it should not be shorter than five minutes nor much longer than ten. In learning to make the examen, it is good to spend a shorter time, and then gradually to lengthen it. Equal time need not be spent on each of the five points of the examen. More or less time can be devoted to each point according to the needs and inspiration of each person.

112

The Particular Examen

"Divide and conquer" was the Roman slogan, and may also be applied to the spiritual life. To concentrate on rooting out all our faults and acquiring all the virtues at once, would be like leaping on a horse and riding off in all directions. We would get nowhere.

A military commander intent on taking an enemy strong point carefully masses his forces and hammers away at the weakest point in the enemy defense. Only by a concentration of forces can he break through. Similarly, in our efforts to preserve and increase the Christ-life within us, we must concentrate on purifying our heart of one sin or fault at a time, on gaining one virtue at a time. This does not mean complete neglect of other imperfections or of other virtues, but it does mean a special, sustained, all-out attack on one objective. This strategy is called the particular examen. It is easily included in the general examination of conscience.

"The axe is laid to the roots," said Saint John the Baptist. The subject of the particular examen should be that root sin or imperfection which is keeping us from closer friendship with our Lord. Taking the positive approach, we concentrate on that virtue which we need most to become holier Catholics. Selection of a subject for the particular examen implies a good knowledge of ourselves, and hence our spiritual director should be consulted. We can be so easily fooled and waste so much time and effort if we do not have the wise and experienced direction of our confessor. Perseverance is needed in being faithful to the particular examen, but from time to time the subject may be changed according to the state and needs of the individual soul. To determine this we should consult the spiritual director.

A very efficient and beneficial method is to mark down in a little book the number of times we have succeeded or failed in the particular examen. This will form a progress chart, and we can compare our efforts from day to day, week to week. This spiritual bookkeeping is recommended only if it is found to be helpful.

Our Attitude toward the Examen

The examen is primarily a prayer and not merely a period of self-examination. It is a conversation with our Lord in which we discuss with Him practical ways of being a better Catholic, a better companion of His and the Blessed Mother. "He who says 'Lord, Lord' shall not enter the kingdom of heaven, but he who does the will of My Father." The examen makes us conscious of living out of love of our Lord and our Lady. Generosity and largeheartedness are the key to making the examen a sure and direct route to a more intimate friendship with our Lord Jesus Christ. Our Lord and Blessed Mother want to enrich our life, to broaden and expand it by use of the examination of conscience.

Examination of Conscience

Act of presence of God: I believe, Lord, that You are with me now, at this time of examination of conscience. ¶ In Your creatures, the works of Your hands, You surround me. ¶ Through sanctifying grace, the divine life, You live within me. ¶ Dear Blessed Mother, you too are always with me, by your tender love, your motherly concern.

Gratitude: As I look over this past day, dear Lord, I find it overflowing with Your blessings. ¶ I do not know where to begin—so many supernatural wonders: my faith, the Blessed Sacrament, Mass, the life of grace; ¶ so many marvelous people: loving parents, my brothers and sisters, my friends; ¶ so many advantages: my country, my education, my health; ¶ so many beauties of nature: the sky, the sunshine, the trees; ¶ so many good times: the fun we have at school, ball games, dances. ¶ Thank You, my heavenly Father, for creating all these gifts, for making the world such a wonderful place. ¶ It was good to be alive today. ¶ Thank You for making me.

Petition for light: Dear Holy Spirit, dwelling in my soul, help me to put the right value on this day: to view God's blessings as His personal gifts, to recognize my troubles as splinters of our Lord's cross, to see my sins and faults for what they are, to see through the tricks of the devil. ¶ Dear Blessed Mother, sorrowing at the foot of the cross, teach me to know Jesus as you do, to know myself as Jesus knows me, to know the malice of sin as you do.

Review of the day

My thoughts: Did I raise my mind to think of our Lord and Blessed Mother in prayer? ¶ Were my thoughts of other people charitable and kind, or did I judge them harshly and without evidence? ¶ Did I keep my mind pure and clean, or did I choose to delay on impure thoughts or images? ¶ Were my thoughts humble, or did I consider myself better than somebody else, just because I am a better athlete, worker, or student? ¶ Did I let discouragement, the special weapon of the devil, prey on my mind merely because I made some mistakes? ¶ Did I have a right intention in all my actions, the glory of God and the help of my neighbor?

My words: Was my speech today proper for a child of our Lady? ¶ Was I encouraging and cheerful in my speech, or sour and sarcastic? ¶ Did I boast and brag about myself? ¶ Did I complain at everything? ¶ Did I damage the good name of another by gossiping about his character? ¶ Were my words always sincere and honest, decent and polite? ¶ Did I praise God reverently in my vocal prayers?

My actions: Did I try to imitate our Lord and His Blessed Mother today? ¶ Did I show love for my parents by gladly obeying and helping them? ¶ Did I perform my study or work lazily, or with diligence and care? ¶ Did I avoid occasions of sin, places and persons I know are not good for me? ¶ Did I show good sportsmanship today? ¶ Did I try to see Christ in others and to help them, or was I selfish? ¶ Did I offer up the hard things of the day in reparation to our Lord's Sacred Heart?

Particular examen: Did I make a real effort to overcome myself in rooting out this one fault or acquiring this one virtue? ¶ How many times did I succeed or fail? ¶ Why did I fail or succeed? ¶ Did I grow discouraged or did I trust in our Lord?

Contrition: Dear Jesus, as I think of You hanging on the cross for love of me, Your strong hands pierced with nails, Your back torn with the scourges, Your eyes pleading for love— ¶ As I think of You in this way I am so sorry for my sins which caused You this suffering. ¶ I am so sorry for my sins because You are so good. ¶ Yes, dear Lord, and I am sorry even for my frequent faults and imperfections. ¶ If I had not been so indulgent with myself, but manfully shouldered the cross, I would have lightened the burden of Your cross just as Simon of Cyrene did for You. ¶ Dear Blessed Mother, standing at the foot of the cross with me, I am sorry for disappointing you and causing you pain.

Resolution: Dear Lord, You and I both know how weak I am; I am not trusting in myself, but in You. ¶ You will have to help me if I am to conquer my heart and give it to You. ¶ Guard me from discouragement. ¶ May I always remember how You, dear Lord, fell three times carrying Your cross. ¶ You did not lie there discouraged and refuse to rise; You struggled on for love of me. ¶ I will carry on for love of You. ¶ Dear Mary, my mother, I trust in your kindness and protection to aid me to serve you and our Lord with greater fidelity tomorrow.

Suggestions for the Particular Examen

The following topics may help indicate subject matter for the particular examen. They are somewhat general and must be adapted to each individual and made more specific by him. In choosing the particular examen, one should first concentrate on any sinful habits, then on the root difficulty which is blocking his spiritual progress. Of course each topic may be approached as a defect to be overcome or a virtue to be achieved.

The particular examen can be changed from time to time or modified as different problems arise. One's spiritual director should be consulted about the choice of a particular examen.

The particular examen should not degenerate into a mechanical routine. It is not a spiritual strait jacket, but a sword and shield in the struggle to follow Christ closely. We follow Christ more closely by examining our conduct toward God, others, and ourselves. In most of these suggestions for a particular examen there is no question of sin involved.

God

Prayer: Fidelity to mental prayer, examen, rosary, morning prayers—discouragement in prayer—making ordinary actions a prayer by a pure intention—being simple and childlike with God, not mechanical and formal.

Reverence: Reverence for God in prayer—at Mass in the Blessed Sacrament—seeing God in others.

Humility: Humility is truth. The realization that any skill, intelligence, or strength I have is a gift of God—neither belittling nor exaggerating the talents or accomplishments I possess.

Obedience: Docility and eagerness to obey the commandments of God—of His Church—attitude of thinking with the Church—prompt obedience to lawful authority.

Reparation: Making up for past sins and negligences—offering prayers, works, joys, sufferings in reparation for the sins of others—special acts of reparation to the Sacred Heart of Jesus.

Trust: Realizing God is interested in everything I do—trusting in His goodness—drawing strength from this confidence in Him.

Others

Courtesy: Following the norms of Christian politeness—expressing gratitude for things done for me—being Christlike toward others.

Speech: Finding good things to say about people—never ruining another's reputation by gossip—speaking kindly and not harshly to others—not being obstinate in conversation.

Fairness: Honesty at work or in games—doing a fair day's work for a fair wage—never passing off somebody else's work for my own.

Generosity: Volunteering when somebody needs help—not waiting to be asked before doing something or expecting to be thanked when it is done—taking an active part in family, class, and parish activities.

Cooperation: Willingness to help others—not trying to dominate—subordinating my own preferences to those of the group—following directions faithfully.

Charity: Seeing Christ in others by focusing on their good qualities—respecting the opinions of others—going out of my way to help one who is sick or in trouble.

Myself

Courage: Acting from a good motive—not doing things because of what others will think of me—defending what I know to be the truth.

Purity: Avoiding persons, places, and literature that may be an occasion of sin—choosing good, wholesome entertainment—keeping myself busy: an idle mind is the devil's workshop—praying to Mary, my mother, for the grace of true purity.

Attitude toward money: Spending money sensibly and not extravagantly—not being stingy—not judging the worth of people by their wealth—not being greedy—using money to make others happy.

Study: Working hard at school—realizing my duty to develop my mind for God, the Church, my country—not being discouraged if I am not a genius—not being proud if I am.

Control of temper: Not letting trifles annoy me: a man is as big as the things which bother him—apologizing (in act at least) to those I may have offended—realizing the give-and-take of life.

Language: Special reverence for God's holy name—avoiding vulgar and improper expressions—never telling or listening to improper stories; prudently directing the conversation to wholesome topics.

An Act of Perfect Contrition

O my God, I believe in You, ¶ I hope in You, ¶ I love You above all things ¶ with all my soul, with all my heart, and with all my strength. ¶ I love You because You are infinitely good and worthy of being loved; ¶ and because I love You I repent with all my heart of having offended You. ¶ Have mercy on me, a sinner. Amen.   [300 days, R. 37]

In Atonement for Daily Neglects

Eternal Father, I offer You the Sacred Heart of Jesus with all its love, all its sufferings, and all its merits:

First, to expiate all the sins I have committed this day and during my life. ¶ Glory be to the Father and to the Son and to the Holy Spirit. Amen.

Second, to purify the good I have done in my poor way this day and during all my life. ¶ Glory be to the Father and to the Son and to the Holy Spirit. Amen.

Third, to make up for the good I ought to have done and that I have neglected this day and during all my life.

Glory be to the Father and to the Son and to the Holy Spirit. Amen.   Stedman

119

Resolution

Adorable Jesus, divine model of that perfection to which we should all aspire, I will endeavor this day to follow Your example, to be mild, humble, chaste, zealous, patient, charitable, and resigned. Dispose my heart to keep Your commandments and to observe with all exactness the obligations of my state of life. I am resolved to watch over myself with the greatest diligence, and to live so that I may always be pleasing to You. I will take care that I may not offend with my tongue. I will turn away my eyes that I may not see sin; and I will be particularly attentive not to fall this day into my accustomed failings, but to struggle against them with Your gracious assistance. Enlighten my mind, purify my heart, and guide my steps, that I may pass all my life serving You faithfully. Amen.

Author unknown

Jesus, Help Me!

In every need let me come to You with humble trust, saying "Jesus, help me!" In all my doubts, perplexities, and temptations "Jesus, help me!" ¶ In hours of loneliness, weariness, and trials "Jesus, help me!" In the failure of my plans and hopes; in disappointments, troubles, and sorrows "Jesus, help me!" ¶ When others fail me, and Your grace alone can assist me "Jesus, help me!" ¶ When I throw myself on Your tender love as a Father and Savior "Jesus, help me!" ¶ When my heart is cast down by failure, at seeing no good come from my efforts "Jesus, help me!" ¶ When I feel impatient, and my cross irritates me "Jesus, help me!" ¶ When I am ill, and my head and hands cannot work and I am lonely "Jesus, help me!" ¶ Always, always, in spite of weakness,

falls, and shortcomings of every kind "Jesus, help me
and never forsake me." Stedman

Act of Confidence

My God, I believe most firmly that You watch over
all who hope in You, and that we can want for
nothing when we rely upon You in all things; therefore I am resolved for the future to have no anxieties
and to cast all my cares upon You. "In peace in the
selfsame I will sleep and I will rest; for You, O
Lord, singularly have settled me in hope."

Men may deprive me of worldly goods and of
honors; sickness may take from me my strength and
the means of serving You; I may even lose Your
grace by sin, but my trust shall never leave me. I
will preserve it till the last moment of my life, and
the powers of hell shall seek in vain to wrest it from
me. "In peace in the selfsame I will sleep and I
will rest."

Let others seek happiness in their wealth, in their
talents; let them trust in the purity of their lives, the
severity of their mortifications, in the number of
their good works, the fervor of their prayers; as for
me, O my God, in my very confidence lies all my
hope. "For You, O Lord, singularly have settled me
in hope." This confidence can never be vain. "No
one has hoped in the Lord and has been confounded."

I am assured, therefore, of my eternal happiness,
for I firmly hope in it and all my hope is in You.
"In You, O Lord, have I hoped; let me never be
confounded."

I know, I know but too well!—that I am frail and
changeable; I know the power of temptation against
the strongest virtue. I have seen stars fall from
heaven, and pillars of the firmament totter; but these

things alarm me not. While I hope in You, I am sheltered from all misfortune, and I am sure that my trust shall endure, for I rely upon You to sustain this unfailing hope.

Finally, I know that my confidence cannot exceed Your bounty, and that I shall never receive less than I have hoped for from You. Therefore I hope that You will sustain me against my evil inclinations, that You will protect me against the most furious assaults of the evil one, and that You will cause my weakness to triumph over my most powerful enemies. I hope that You will never cease to love me, and that I shall love You unceasingly. "In You, O Lord, have I hoped; let me never be confounded."

Blessed Claude de la Colombiere

You are the salt of the earth; but if the salt loses its strength, what shall it be salted with?
Matthew 5:13

☦ Confession

Mortal sin is a direct "No!" to My challenge.
It is a turning away from God—
a surrender to the enemy.
Sin drives grace from the soul.
The sinner, refusing My example, tells God,
"Not Your will, but mine be done."
To all who put aside God's will for their own I can but repeat:

How is it that you call Me, "Master, Master,"
and will not do what I bid you?

Is it any wonder when you sin
that you should experience deep dissatisfaction,
flowing from the knowledge that you betrayed Me?
Many seek to lose their sense of guilt
in the distractions that modern amusements afford.
But always, when they are forced to pause
and be alone with their thoughts,
their sense of guilt returns.
They long for pardon and for peace.
They long for sanctifying grace.

"Why are you sad, O my soul
and disturbed within me?
Hope in God,
for I shall praise him once again,
my Savior and my God" (Psalm 41:12).

In these words of David is the answer
to the great unhappiness of mankind.
For to souls bent low under the weight of sin,
to souls uneasy in their repentance,
to souls anxious to be assured of God's forgiveness,
He sent Me,
His only-begotten Son,
the Savior.
In My life on earth
I constantly warned men of their punishment
if they did not repent.
And just as constantly I showed that I had the
    power to forgive sins.
Never before had anyone said,
as I said to Mary Magdalene,
"Your sins are forgiven you."

123

Because their sins had hardened their hearts
there were some who refused to accept
My offer of pardon and peace.
But to all who came with love and with sorrow,
to Mary Magdalene, to Peter,
to the man paralyzed in body and soul,
to all these I repeated My message,
your faith has saved you; go in peace.

This power I passed on to My Church.
On Easter night when the apostles gathered in
the upper room
I appeared in their midst.
I gave them the power to forgive sins.
Peace be upon you:
I came upon an errand from My Father,
and now am sending you out in My turn. . . .
Receive the Holy Spirit;
when you forgive men's sins they are forgiven,
when you hold them bound, they are held bound.
In passing on My power to these men
and their successors, My priests,
I have made it possible for you
to kneel at My feet as did Mary Magdalene
and share in the joy of pardon
and know the meaning of peace.

But the sacrament of penance is more than
forgiveness.
It is a divine medicine.
I am the great physician of souls.
When you come to Me,
when you confess your sins and faults,
I give you the medicine of My grace
to make you strong in those very things in which
you are weak.

If you are frequently uncharitable,
I will help you to see Me in your fellow man.
If you are disrespectful to parents and teachers,
I will help you see My authority in them.
If you are troubled by impure thoughts,
I will help you turn your attention to something else.
When you confess a sin or fault to Me
it is as if we two had made a contract.
You, by mentioning the sin or fault,
receive My promise of sufficient grace to overcome
　　it next time.

The price I ask you to pay for this great sacrament
is small indeed.
All I ask is true contrition.
True contrition is honest
and it is sincere.
You are honest if you tell your sins as you see them,
not excusing them, not exaggerating them,
not being "scrupulous."
You are sincere if you resolve not to commit
　　these sins again.
No matter how much you fear falling again,
you are sincere as long as you here and now can say,
"I am resolved not to do that again."

A measure of your honesty and sincerity
is to choose a regular confessor
to whom your conscience is an open book.
Tell him all your sins and faults and trials.
Listen to his advice,
follow it out carefully.
Choose a man for whom you have great respect
and a man in whom you have complete confidence.
Then deal with him as you would with Me,
for in truth it is I who am directing you.

Love this sacrament of pardon and peace.
It is one of the chief weapons I have given
to those who wish to accept My challenge.

It is the ordinary means for regaining grace,
the Christ-life,
when lost by mortal sin.
Without sanctifying grace your soul is a setting
    without its jewel.
But with it you are
a brother of My saints,
a son of My Mother,
a tabernacle of My Holy Spirit,
a member of My mystical body,
and a child of God.

The Confession

Preparation: Penance is a sacrament. If we remember this, we will be less likely to hurry in and out of the church and the confessional, barely fulfilling the requirements for a good confession. On the other hand, we should avoid becoming scrupulous and not spend undue time in confessing and especially in the examination of conscience.

Even if we have never committed a mortal sin we should approach the sacrament in deep humility. In the best of us there will arise venial sins and faults and imperfections that catch us off our guard. We should attempt to eliminate them from our lives. To do so is part of the challenge of Christlike living.

Examination of conscience for confession: Beg, first of all, the light of the Holy Spirit in your examination.

We should call on our Lady, our guardian angel, and our patron saints to help us make a good confession.

In examining our conscience we should keep in mind:

We are obliged to confess only mortal sins. We must confess all mortal sins committed since our last good confession.

Mortal sins left out of a previous confession through forgetfulness should be confessed as such. Mortal sins left out of a previous confession purposely must be confessed as such, as well as all mortal sins committed since the last good confession.

To be mortal a sin must be a serious matter, and this you will know from instruction; must be committed after sufficient reflection, and this means we are aware that it is a serious matter (the reflection may take only a second), and that we are free to do it or not to do it; and we must have full consent of our will. (Anything done when we are taken by surprise, or when we are not fully awake, for instance, does not constitute a mortal sin.)

If one is in doubt about whether or not he has committed a serious sin, he is under no strict obligation to confess it. It would be advisable, however, except for a scrupulous person, to mention the matter as doubtful in the next confession.

In confessing venial sins it is often better to select a few for which we are sincerely sorry than to recite a whole catalogue of offenses for which we may not have true contrition or a firm purpose of amendment. It is also wise, though not necessary, to examine the causes behind these sins or faults and to mention them in confession. For example:

I told a lie because I did not want to seem to be in the wrong.

I told an off-color joke because I wanted to attract the attention of others to myself.

I was late for Mass because I delayed to talk unnecessarily with a friend on the way.

Ordinarily the examination of conscience for a person who has been faithful to his daily examinations of conscience should not take more than five or six minutes.

In examining our consciences we must remember that there is a difference between temptation and sin. Temptation is an invitation to sin. We do no wrong unless we say "yes" to the invitation. Temptation may be permitted by God to strengthen us and add to our merits. The more frequently we have resisted a certain temptation, the less likely we are to give in on future occasions. The duration of the temptation does not matter. It may plague us all day and still remain just a temptation. Only when we consciously and deliberately give in does the temptation become a sin.

A general confession of our past life or of the time since our last general confession is advised occasionally for those who are trying to become more Christlike. In examining our conscience for a general confession, we do not have to list in detail the sins and faults committed. A general examination of the more persistent sins and faults is sufficient.

THE TEN COMMANDMENTS

First Commandment: I am the Lord Thy God, thou shalt not have strange gods before Me.

Idolatry. Belief in superstitions (Spiritism, Ouija board, fortunetelling). Superstitious practices. Sacrilege against persons, places, or things consecrated to God. Lying in confession.

Second Commandment: Thou shalt not take the name of the Lord Thy God in vain.

Blasphemy (speaking in contempt or scorn of God and holy things). Cursing (wishing moral or physical evils on someone). Oaths and vows without good and sufficient reason.

Third Commandment: Remember that thou keep holy the Sabbath.

Missing Mass on Sundays and holydays without sufficient reason. Doing unnecessary servile work on Sundays and holydays.

Fourth Commandment: Honor thy father and thy mother.

Violations of love and respect for parents. Disobedience to parents. Disobedience to any who have legitimate authority. Disrespect for authority. Disrespect for just laws.

Fifth Commandment: Thou shalt not kill.

Murder. Suicide. Culpable disregard for one's health. Overindulgence in food or drink. Vengeance. Envy and hatred. Anger. Occasion of sin for another. Co-operation in the sin of another.

Sixth Commandment: Thou shalt not commit adultery.
Ninth Commandment: Thou shalt not covet thy neighbor's wife.

Impure acts or touches with myself or another. Entertaining impure thoughts or desires. Attending bad shows. Reading bad books. Impure talk and jokes. Immodesty in dress or action.

Seventh Commandment: Thou shalt not steal.
Tenth Commandment: Thou shalt not covet thy neighbor's goods.

Stealing. Excessive gambling. Envy of another's wealth, talents, or good fortune. Not paying just debts. Serious carelessness with another's goods. Unjust damaging of another's goods.

Eighth Commandment: Thou shalt not bear false witness against thy neighbor.

Lying. Revealing hidden faults or defects. Rash judgments about another's actions or intentions. Attributing false sins or defects to another. Violations of secrets.

COMMANDMENTS OF THE CHURCH

1 Attend Mass and refrain from servile work on Sundays and holydays.
2 Fast and abstain on the days appointed.
3 Confess your sins at least once a year if guilty of mortal sin.
4 Receive Communion once a year during the Easter season.
5 Contribute to the support of your pastor.

Contrition and amendment: When we have finished our examination of conscience we should make an act of contrition.

We should strive to have perfect contrition in all our confessions. Perfect contrition is sorrow for sin because we have offended God who is perfect love. It is better than imperfect contrition, which is sorrow for sin because we fear God's punishment, hell. Imperfect contrition is sufficient for a good confession. The Catholic will, of course, try to make his sorrow for sin more and more perfect by meditating on the greatness and goodness of God, and his own littleness and ingratitude. We should not, however, completely reject the motive of fear of hell. It will act as a safeguard against sin, should our love of God grow cold.

Just as contrition does not depend on feelings but on the intellectual admission of our wrongdoing and the will to ask for forgiveness, so too a firm purpose of amendment does not mean that we feel any stronger, but that we desire here and now never to offend our Lord again by sin.

Acknowledging our weakness, and placing ourselves in the hands of Christ, we should seek to make our purpose of amendment more firm by thinking briefly on the motives, natural and supernatural, that will keep us from sinning again.

The manner of confessing: After our preparation is completed we should make our confession, using the following form or one like it:

Bless me, Father. I have sinned; my last confession was . . . ago. Since that time I have committed the following sins: *(give the number of times, at least for the mortal sins)*. I am sorry for these sins and for the sins of my past life, particularly for . . . *(mention some past sin for which you are especially sorry)*.

Listen to the counsel the priest may want to give you. Do not hesitate to ask advice if you do not understand what he has said. Then, repeat your act of contrition. As you do so the priest will say the prayer of absolution:

May our Lord Jesus Christ absolve you; and I by His authority, do absolve you, from every bond of excommunication and interdict as far as I am able, and you

130

have need. Therefore, I absolve you of your sins, in the name of the Father and of the Son and of the Holy Spirit. Amen.

And in the name of the Church, he says:

May the Passion of our Lord Jesus Christ, may the merits of the Blessed Virgin Mary and all the saints, may the good you do and the evil you may endure, profit you for the remission of sins, the increase of grace and glory in the life without end. Amen.

Other prayers usually said by the priest are:

May the Lord be in your heart and on your lips that you may properly confess all your sins in the name of the Father and of the Son and of the Holy Spirit. Amen.

May God almighty have mercy on you, forgive you your sins, and bring you to life everlasting. Amen.

May the almighty and merciful Lord grant you pardon, absolution, and remission of all your sins. Amen.

Penance and thanksgiving: After leaving the confessional always say your penance as soon as possible, to avoid the possibility of forgetting what you are to do. Ordinarily you should complete it before receiving Holy Communion. Be exact, but not scrupulous in performing your penance, neither adding to nor subtracting from the prayers to be said.

PRAYERS BEFORE CONFESSION

Prayers for Light

Come, Holy Spirit, and fill the hearts of Your faithful, and kindle in them the fire of Your love. ¶ Send forth Your Spirit and they shall be created; and You shall renew the face of the earth.

Let us pray. O God, who by the light of the Holy Spirit, did instruct the hearts of the faithful, grant us by the same Spirit to relish what is right and ever to rejoice in His consolation, through Christ our Lord. Amen.   [5 years, R. 287]

Come, O Holy Spirit, divine Spirit of light and truth, assist me to discover my sins, to be truly sorry for them, to confess them sincerely, and amend my life. Amen.

Reflections

I know, O Lord, that, according to the greatness of the person offended, the greater is the offence. Yet I do not fear to offend Thee, the infinite God. To sin is to insult Thee in the grossest of all conceivable ways. This then, O my soul! is what the sinfulness of sin consists in. It is lifting up my hand against my infinite Benefactor, against my Almighty Creator, Preserver and Judge—against Him in whom all majesty and glory and beauty and reverence and sanctity center; against the one only God.

My God, I confess that before now I have utterly forgotten this, and that I am continually forgetting it! I have acted many a time as if I were my own master, and turned from Thee rebelliously. I have acted according to my own pleasure, not according to Thine. I do not understand how dreadful sin is—and I do not hate it, and fear it, as I ought. I have no horror of it, or loathing. I do not turn from it with indignation, as being an insult to Thee, but I trifle with it, and, even if I do not commit great sins, I have no great reluctance to do small ones. O my God, what a great and awful difference is there between what I am and what I ought to be.

Imagine you see Jesus Christ on the Cross, and say to Him with the penitent thief, "Lord, remember me when Thou shalt come into Thy kingdom"; that is, "Remember me Lord, in mercy, remember not my sins, but Thine own cross; remember Thine own sufferings, remember that Thou sufferedst for me, a sinner; remember in the last day that I, during my lifetime, felt Thy sufferings, that I suffered on my cross by Thy side. Remember me then, and make me remember Thee now." Amen.

Cardinal Newman

Act of Contrition

O my God, I am heartily sorry for having offended You, ¶ and I detest all my sins, because I dread the loss of heaven and the pains of hell, ¶ but most of all, because I have offended You, my God, who are all good and deserving of all my love. ¶ I firmly resolve, by the help of Your grace, to confess my sins, do penance, and amend my life. Amen.

[3 years, R. 36]

Prayer of Contrition

My God, my Creator, my Master, my friend and lover, my judge, ¶ almighty yet all-merciful, all angry yet all-loving, all just yet all-seeing, ¶ this evil thing I have done, evil in itself, evil in its degrading consequences, evil in its offensiveness to You, ¶ for You have forbidden it, You detest it, it violates Your law, Your order, it in some way hurts You, ¶ I have done this thing, I deserve the consequences, I have no excuse, Father, forgive me. ¶ I have offended You, the creature the Creator, the slave the master, the beloved the lover, the culprit the judge. ¶ I deserve the consequences. ¶ I have no excuses, Father, forgive me. ¶ I have offended You, the son the Father, the brother the Brother, I have crucified Your Son, Jesus. I deserve the consequences. ¶ I have no excuse, Father, forgive me. ¶ I wish I had not done it, for my own sake, for the sake of others, but most for Your sake, for the sake of Jesus Christ. ¶ I have hurt Him, hurt Him in His tender heart. ¶ It shall not happen again, with Your help it shall not, though my evil nature craves, though my weakness fears. ¶ I am determined, for my own sake, for Your sake more than mine. ¶ I will take the means to keep it far from me, to avoid the danger, to put it out of my life, and all that leads to it; but I am needy and poor, O God, help me. Amen.

Archbishop Goodier

Prayer for Confidence

I come to You, O Jesus, as a sick man to his physician in hope of obtaining a cure. You said that those who are afflicted with disease should approach the one who is able and willing to help them. And so I come to You because You are that one. I cry out with the leper in the Gospel: "Lord, if You desire, You can make me clean."

Inspire me with the same holy confidence with which the sick during Your lifetime presented themselves before You. And grant that, like them, I may say within myself, if I but touch the hem of His garment I will be healed. With like confidence, I approach and cast myself at Your feet and beg pardon for all the sins of my whole life which I detest from my heart for the love of You.

The Miserere, Psalm 50

The *Miserere*, David's song of repentance and hope, is the traditional prayer of penance in the liturgy of the Church.

Have mercy on me, O God, according to your mercy; according to your great clemency blot out my iniquity.

Wash me completely from my guilt, and cleanse me from my sin.

134

For I acknowledge my iniquity, and my sin is always before me.

Against you only have I sinned, and I have done what is evil in your sight.

This I confess that you may be known to be just in your sentence, right in your judgment.

Behold, I was born in guilt, and my mother conceived me in sin.

Behold, you delight in sincerity of heart, and teach me wisdom in the depths of my soul.

Sprinkle me with hyssop, that I may be cleansed; wash me, that I may become whiter than snow.

Let me hear sounds of joy and gladness, let the bones which you have crushed rejoice.

Turn away your face from my sins, and blot out all my guilt.

Create a clean heart for me, O God, and renew in me a steadfast spirit.

Cast me not off from your presence, and take not your holy spirit from me.

Restore to me the joy of your salvation, and strengthen me with a generous spirit.

I will teach the unjust your ways, and sinners shall be converted to you.

Deliver me from blood-guilt, O God, God my savior; let my tongue rejoice because of your justice.

O Lord, open my lips, and my mouth shall declare your praise.

For you do not delight in sacrifice; and a burnt-offering you would not accept, if I offered it.

My sacrifice, O God, is a contrite spirit, a contrite and humbled heart, O God, you will not despise.

In your goodness, O Lord, deal kindly with Sion, that you may rebuild the wall of Jerusalem.

Then will you accept lawful sacrifices, oblations and burnt-offerings, then will they offer bullocks on your altar.

Motives for Amendment

God loves me. He made me to know, love, and serve Him here and be happy with Him in heaven. By sin I offend this loving God.

Jesus Christ, the Son of God, Second Person of the Blessed Trinity, became man, lived, suffered, and died for me. He made it possible for me to get to heaven. When I sin I reject His love and grace.

When I do wrong I betray and disappoint our Lady, my mother, who loves me as her own child.

When I sin I am a coward. I surrender to the world, or to the devil, or to my own baser instincts. When I resist temptation I am Christlike.

Sins and faults, even the smallest, weaken me and make me more vulnerable. Unless I fight courageously, I will slip into bigger, more frequent faults and sins.

Let me always have a holy fear of hell, and beg God for a clearer idea of the terrible punishment that waits for those who die in the state of mortal sin.

Ejaculations for Deeper Contrition

My God, I am truly sorry for my sins and I firmly resolve to sin no more. [3 years, R. 36]

O convert us to You, that we may be thankful, humble, and devout; for You are our salvation, our power, and our strength.

Jesus, son of David, have mercy on me.
[500 days, R. 73]

O God, you know my foolishness, and my faults are
not hidden from you. Psalm 68:6

The Lord is my light and my salvation: whom shall
I fear? The Lord is the defense of my life: whom
shall I dread? Psalm 26:1

Hear, O Lord, my voice which cries to you, be gracious to me and answer me. Psalm 26:7

PRAYERS AFTER CONFESSION

Thanksgiving for God's Mercy,
Psalm 102

Bless the Lord, O my soul, and let my whole being
bless his holy name.

Bless the Lord, O my soul, and forget not all his
benefits, who forgives all your faults, who heals all
your infirmities, who redeems your life from destruc-
tion, who crowns you with grace and mercy, who
fills your life with good things: your youth is renewed like the eagle's.

The Lord performs works of justice, and renders
justice to all the oppressed.

He made known his ways to Moses, his deeds to the
children of Israel.

The Lord is merciful and gracious, slow to anger
and abounding in kindness.

He will not always contend, nor will he be angry
forever.

He does not deal with us according to our sins, nor
repay us according to our faults.

For as high as heaven is above the earth, so great is
his goodness toward those who fear him; as far as

the east is from the west, so far has he removed our offenses from us.

As a father has compassion on his children, so the Lord has compassion on those who fear him.

For he knows the stuff of which we are made: he remembers that we are dust.

Man's days are as grass; like the flower of the field so does he flourish; scarcely does the wind pass over it and it is gone; and its place knows it no more.

But the goodness of the Lord is forever and ever toward those who fear him, and his justice toward children's children, toward those who keep his covenant, and are mindful of his precepts, to observe them.

The Lord has established his throne in heaven, and his sovereignty is supreme.

Bless the Lord, all his angels, mighty in strength, you who do his bidding, in order to comply with his command.

Bless the Lord, all you his hosts, his servants, who do his will.

Bless the Lord, all you his works, in all the places of his dominion, bless the Lord, O my soul.

Reflections on Grace

Thy grace can undo the past, it can realize the hopeless. No sinner, ever so odious, but may become a Saint; no Saint, ever so exalted, but has been, or might have been, a sinner. Grace overcomes nature, and grace only overcomes it.

Thy grace triumphed in Magdalen, in Matthew, and in Nicodemus; heavenly grace came down upon corrupt human nature; it subdued impurity in the youthful woman, covetousness in the publican, fear of man in the Pharisee.

The rebellion of my reason, the waywardness of my feelings, the disorder of my thoughts, the fever of passion, the treachery of my senses,—these evils may Thy all-powerful grace subdue in me. Amen.

Cardinal Newman

Prayer of Petition

May this confession, O Lord, by the merits of Blessed Mary, ever virgin, Your mother, and of all the saints, be pleasing and acceptable in Your sight. Let Your goodness and mercy supply for whatever has been wanting in my contrition, and in the purity and integrity of my confession. Grant, in Your mercy, to consider me perfectly and entirely absolved in heaven, who lives and reigns God, world without end. Amen.

Author unknown

You, however, are a chosen race, a royal priesthood, a holy nation, a purchased people.

1 Peter 2:9

The Mass

✝

From the beginning of time
men gathered together eager to worship God
    as He deserved;
to give God a gift that was worthy of Him;
a gift
which would carry all their desire to God;

which would express the yearning in their hearts,
the hunger in their souls;
which said,
we worship You and thank You,
we are sorry we have done what You would not like,
we want Your favor and friendship and love,
we want to give ourselves to You,
to be united to You.

But men could devise no means
to worship God as He deserved,
to adore and thank Him,
to make up for sin,
to bring union or favor or friendship or love.
For men had nothing that was worthy of God,
only grain from the fields,
only animals from the flocks.
They could not even give themselves,
for they were sinners.

And then I came down on earth and offered My gift,
a gift of infinite value.
This was Myself,
My own life,
offered and surrendered to God.
This is the greatest love a man can show,
that he should lay down his life for his friends.
I gave Myself willingly
and let men nail My body to a cross
and pour out My blood upon the ground,
that you might raise your heads
and walk the earth as free men,
free from sin and the power of sin in your souls,
free to love God and to be friends with God,
free to have a life above mere human life,
to share and increase by grace in the life of God.

With this perfect sacrifice of Mine
everything was achieved.
In the name of every human being I offered to God
the perfect gift,
the gift which worshiped Him as He deserved.

Yet I was not satisfied.
My sacrifice was not for the human race in general;
it was for each in particular:
for you and your neighbors down the street,
for the housekeeper with her market bag,
for the stenographer with her notebook,
for the executive with his office,
for the laborer with his shovel.

You were all one with Me now,
sharing My own divine life,
forming for Me a mystical body,
a new organism to carry on My work among men.
That is why My sacrifice on Calvary,
even though it expiated everything,
even though it merited everything,
was not enough for Me.
Because it was for each of you that I died,
I wanted to come into your everyday lives,
I wanted to satisfy the craving in your hearts
    for a visible sacrifice,
thus uniting you closer to each other
and closer to Myself.
I wanted to put My one great sacrifice into
    your hands
so that it might become your sacrifice,
that you might give this gift of Mine over and
    over again,
uniting your little gifts with My great gift,
that we might give together.

And so I did what you would never dare to imagine,
I caused My body given for you
and My blood shed for you
to begin existing in a new manner
as a sacrament,
as a sign which effects what it signifies.
On the night before I died
I changed bread and wine into My body and blood,
and by this separate consecration
I not only signified My death the following day
on the cross
but I actually made that bloody sacrifice
truly present in an unbloody manner
and thus offered it up to the Father.
I then communicated My gift to My apostles
as a sign of its acceptance by the Father
and of the union between us all
which it had effected at last.

"Do this in commemoration of Me," I commanded.
Thus did I give to My priests
the power to do just what I had done,
to offer My sacrifice of the cross in an
     unbloody manner
on all the altars of the world
through all ages
till the end of time.
Now I no longer act alone.
I have given My sacrifice to My Church,
to each and every member of My mystical body.
It is your sacrifice now,
uniting you all together in one act of worship
and applying to your individual souls
the riches of grace I won on the cross.
I no longer offer Myself in My physical body
as on Calvary.

Now it is through you,
the members of My mystical body,
that I offer My gift to God.
And the gift that I give is no longer Myself alone,
but all the members of My body united to Me.
And since I now offer My sacrifice through you,
it is you who must do the offering.

How great is My desire that you understand this.
The Mass is not merely offered by the priest for you,
or at your request,
or in your presence.
The Mass is not something you watch
but something you take part in.
It is you who offer the Mass with the priest,
and it is yourselves that you offer.
The Mass is your Mass.
The Mass does not belong to the priest alone.
It belongs also to you,
for you too have a certain share in My priesthood.
You can join with the priest's offering.

Listen to My vicar, Pius XI: ". . . we must bring
together, in the august sacrifice of the Blessed
Eucharist, the act of immolation made by the priest
with that of the Faithful, so that they, too,
        may offer
themselves up as 'a living sacrifice, holy, pleasing
to God.'"

Hear also My vicar, Pius XII: "By the waters
of baptism, as by a common title, Christians
are made members of the mystical body of Christ
the priest; and by the character which is imprinted
on their souls they are appointed to the worship
        of God.

Thus they participate according to their condition
in the priesthood of Christ."

Now you see your highest dignity,
your "lay priesthood."
The ordained priest has a fuller share in
    My priesthood,
his is the power to consecrate,
to make My sacrifice present on the altar.
But yours is the power
to offer that sacrifice with him
once it is present before you.

This, then, is My challenge to you.
Each and every morning of your lives
live up to the dignity to which you are called.

Exercise the power that is yours:
offering My holy sacrifice with the priest.
Exercise your power to believe, so that with eyes
    of faith
you will see Me on the altar,
just as the priest with fingers of faith
holds Me in his hands.

Never waste a Mass.
Never come to church to sit and to watch,
but always to give and to do;
to give with Me a gift that surpasses all gifts,
to do with Me a deed that redeems a world.

See to it that nothing you do be lost or
    wasted for eternity,
all the utterly unimportant things,
all the remorseless round of daily toil.
See that you give to them all a value

144

tremendously deep
by giving them through Me to the Father,
by letting Me present them as part of My gift,
as part of Myself.

Give yourselves to Me at Mass,
enabling Me to offer to the Father My mystical body,
which is the Church.
Give yourselves to each other at Mass,
growing in a union of hearts with one Heart
through a union of gifts with one gift.
Give yourselves at Mass to be other Christs,
other victims,
placing yourselves on the golden paten
next to the bread that will become My body,
pouring your life into the chalice
along with the wine that will become My blood,
bringing to Me all your joys and sorrows,
hopes and fears and gratitude
of a whole day of living.

The Mass is yours!

Only come each morning with faith
and a desire to give.
If these are strong
then your Mass also will be strong,
strong in its power for good,
strong in its blessing for you and those you love,
strong with the strength of the gift you give
and strong with the strength of the deed you do,
strong with the strength of God.

The Prologue

The Mass is an exchange of gifts with God. It is introduced therefore in the same way as an exchange of gifts among men: by an exchange of words. The introductory conversation with God aims at preparing us for the Offertory. It puts us in the right frame of mind, stimulates our desire to give, and crystallizes our feelings of adoration, thanksgiving, sorrow, and petition. The prologue is known as the Mass of the Catechumens. This is because the unbaptized had to leave before the Offertory, for they were not yet part of Christ's mystical body and so had no power to offer Christ's sacrifice.

The Offertory

Every gift has two elements: its meaning and its value. A gift may have great meaning but little value, such as the widow's mite in the Gospel. Likewise there may be great value in a gift but little meaning. Now as Mass begins there is on the altar the visible gift of bread and wine which of itself has neither meaning nor value. At the Offertory the priest presents this gift to God and tells Him that it signifies and carries the offering "of all here present and of all faithful Christians." Here then is a gift capable of representing the combined offerings of every member of the mystical body of Christ, all the love and gratitude, resolutions, work, and suffering in the heart of each individual soul. Every Catholic is now represented on the altar who has a desire to give something to God. Without such a desire he will not be helping to offer this sacrifice. He will prevent the bread and wine from representing the combined offering of all God's family.

What will the bread and wine represent as far as we are concerned? That depends entirely on us. This gift will signify all we wish to give God on a particular day if we put that meaning into it. It will mean ourselves if we make it mean ourselves. Hence the Offertory is a time of intense activity on our part. It is the psychological moment which decides our active participation in the Mass. The form of our offering will be determined largely by the duties of our everyday lives. Besides devotion to our daily work, it will represent a blind acceptance of every joy and difficulty and failure which God sends us that day. Above all it should include an awareness of the needs and miseries of a whole world, for we cannot offer ourselves to God without offering ourselves to mankind. Our gift now has meaning.

The Consecration

At the Consecration this gift, already so full of meaning, now receives an incomparable value. For Christ our Lord, through the words of His priest, changes the bread and wine into His most precious body and blood. Christ becomes present now as the Victim of Calvary, and the value of His sacrifice on the cross, the deed that shook the world, now becomes the value of our gift. Thus in a true sense we offer again the same sacrifice which Christ offered, signified now and made present by the separate consecration of bread and wine.

But while our Lord is giving new value to our gift, so that it becomes our Gift, He is also giving it a new meaning. Our gift is much more than the outward expression of our interior devotion. For in giving Himself to be offered by us and in becoming the bearer of our interior offering to God, our Lord in this very act unites His devotion to our own, blending them together into one single offering. Our gift now becomes the outward expression of our interior sacrifice united to our Lord's interior sacrifice on Calvary. Thus not only the value of our gift becomes transfigured, but also its meaning. While ennobling our gift, Christ also ennobles our self-offering. The spiritual union of Christ with His members in the act of self-surrender to God: here is the real mystery of the Mass.

And here too is the principle of limitation in the Mass. For since our Lord gives Himself to be offered by His Church, the value of every Mass will depend upon the combined charity and devotion of all the individual members of His mystical body. Christ's personal sacrifice was infinite, but His sacrifice through His members is not. And at Mass it is our gift which He covers with the gold of His own offering. It is our gift which He presents to the Father. Each of us then will draw upon the treasure of the cross for our own needs in proportion to our own capacity, namely the intensity of our love and the sincerity of our surrender at the Offertory.

The Communion

We have now offered the Victim of Calvary, and our self-surrender has gone up to God in union with that of Christ. Holy Communion is God's answer to our action. At the Consecration it was through Christ that we sought union with God; at Communion it is through Christ that God unites us to Himself by giving us a share of the gift we have just offered Him. As a sacrificial meal, as the eating of the victim offered to God, Communion is an integral part of the Mass, for it completes the sacrifice by an exchange of gifts, a return-gift on the part of God. This is why the priest is bound to receive at Mass, so that God's return-gift is always accepted by someone. If it is not accepted by us also, then the Mass is incomplete as far as we are concerned. We are missing the most precious gift and blessing of all.

The full meaning of Communion, however, is not conveyed by the mere physical union between Christ and ourselves. Its most precious aspect is its spiritual significance, the action of Christ in our souls. For He is present in order to communicate His life to us. And while He could accomplish this merely by an act of His will without being present at all, He comes in Communion that we may have a visible sign of the grace He is giving, that we may know He is working in our souls. Nor does His grace unite us to Him only. Just as in our sacrifice we have become united to the whole Church in a collective offering, so in Communion, by receiving a fuller share in the life of Christ, we are more intimately united with all the members of His body. Vivified by His body and blood, we become in a new sense brothers in Christ.

The Epilogue

After Communion the Mass comes swiftly to a close. But since God has accepted our offering and taken possession of us through Christ, He Himself remains with us even though the Mass ends—sacramentally for a certain time and the rest of our day through the sanctifying grace He has increased in our souls. Not only does He shape our own lives now with each passing hour, but through us He reaches the world in which we live. Our lives must correspond therefore to our self-oblation. All our apostolic work for Christ, all our efforts to spread the kingdom of God must draw their inspiration and success from the offering we have made early at Mass. For grace has now made us Christ-bearers, other Christs. "I live, now not I but Christ lives in me." The day by day life of the lay apostle thus becomes a natural continuation of His Mass.

I PRAY THE PARTS OF THE MASS

I Talk to God

PRAYERS AT THE FOOT OF THE ALTAR

My Lord Jesus Christ, ¶ the cross is the symbol of Your life, of Your sacrifice on Calvary. ¶ How fitting it is then for me to begin the liturgy of Your sacrifice with the symbol of Your sacrifice. ¶ Ever so reverently I begin, "In the name of the Father . . ." ¶ In the words of the psalmist I ask for Your light and Your truth. ¶ With these I will be fortified to approach Your altar. ¶ But my heart must be pure, spotless. ¶ In deep humility I confess my sinfulness. ¶ Three times I strike my breast, "Through my fault . . ." ¶ Now, united in spirit with the priest and strengthened by Your grace, I ascend to the Holy of Holies. ¶ My Lord, cleanse all sin from my heart and soul.

149

This is the first prayer of the Mass liturgy that changes with the calendar, with the liturgical season of the year. ¶ It sets the mood of the Mass like music before a play, ¶ like the first few pages of a book. ¶ Lord, help me to capture its spirit, and flood my life with its message.

KYRIE AND GLORIA

"Lord have mercy! Christ have mercy!" ¶ a brief, powerful expression of my dependence on You. ¶ This plea for mercy originated in the Near East and was brought to Europe by pilgrims from the Holy Land. ¶ "Lord have mercy on us! Christ have mercy on us!"

"Glory to God on high . . ." ¶ This joyful hymn is sung or recited on all festive days. ¶ What pure praise I voice to You in this hymn. ¶ For Your own glory I praise You: ¶ "We give You thanks for Your great glory."

GREETING AND COLLECT

The priest turns to me: "The Lord be with you!" ¶ I answer or the server answers for me: "And with your spirit!" ¶ a sign of union between me and the priest. ¶ Backed by my response the priest now sings or reads aloud the official prayer of Your Church, of Your mystical body. ¶ Like the Introit, it changes from day to day and reflects the character of each day's liturgy. ¶ How powerful a prayer! ¶ "Where there are two or more gathered . . ." ¶ Here there are thousands all the world over to answer their *Amen* to this prayer. ¶ Lord Jesus, I join my *Amen* to theirs.

God Talks to Me

READING AND GRADUAL

Most frequently the Reading is from one of Saint Paul's letters. ¶ Sometimes it is a selection from the Old Testament. ¶ But it is always an instruction for me. ¶ Help me to attend to it carefully. ¶ Help me to apply its teaching to my own life.

The Gradual gets its name from the *gradus* or step from which this verse was intoned in the early Church. ¶ Now it is a steppingstone from the Reading to the Gospel. ¶ Like the Introit it echoes the mood of the day's liturgy.

GOSPEL

. . . the word of God. ¶ With the thumb of my right hand I trace a cross on my forehead: Your word will guide my thoughts; ¶ a cross on my lips: Your word will guide my tongue; ¶ a cross on my heart: Your word will rule my heart. ¶ During the Gospel I stand. ¶ I am all attention to Your word. ¶ "If you hear My word, you will be disciples of the truth and the truth shall make you free."

CREED AND OFFERTORY VERSE

On certain feasts the Church bids me make a solemn profession of my faith. ¶ Faith will move mountains. ¶ The apostles described the early Christians: "By faith they became heroes in conflict; by faith subdued kingdoms . . . quenched the violence of fire . . . strong in faith their spirit did not succumb." ¶ Lord, I believe, help my unbelief.

After the greeting, the priest recites the Offertory Verse. ¶ It re-echoes the Introit-Gradual theme. ¶ It introduces the great action that follows.

I Help Put Meaning into the Gift

OFFERING OF BREAD AND WINE

The priest raises the host in offering. ¶ It is pure white bread made from the wheat of the fields. ¶ But it is sacred bread, sacred with the meaning I give it. ¶ It stands for me, for all I want it to stand for: ¶ my prayers, works, ¶ my joys, sufferings. ¶ The priest offers "this spotless host" to the Father for his own numberless sins, offenses, negligences ¶ "and for all here present," ¶ "also for all faithful Christians living and dead . . . as a means of salvation."

Then he adds a few drops of water to the chalice of wine. ¶ The wine represents You, my Lord. ¶ The water, me, Your chosen one. ¶ In sacrifice we are united.

The priest says *offerimus*—we offer." ¶ He voices the prayer of the whole Church, especially those at Mass. ¶ When You offer Yourself, the members of Your mystical body must be offered together with You. ¶ My part is to join in this offering with the priest. ¶ Lord Jesus, I do join in this offering, ¶ help me to make my offering ever more perfect.

ORATE FRATRES

The priest calls me to join him in common prayer that our common sacrifice may be more pleasing to God. ¶ Priest and people, bound together, in offering bread and wine, ¶ in offering themselves.

SECRET

The Secret changes from day to day and echoes the theme of the day's liturgy. ¶ It is part of the Offertory. ¶ It combines a petition, ¶ an offering, ¶ a repetition of the day's theme. ¶ I join myself with the prayer of the Church; ¶ I ask of God with complete confidence what the Church asks of God.

God Puts Value and New Meaning into the Gift

PREFACE

A preface is an introduction, a preparation for what is to come. ¶ The Preface of the Mass introduces the Canon and the Consecration. ¶ The Preface bids me thank my heavenly Father always and everywhere. ¶ It is through You that I thank Him. ¶ It is through You that His greatness is extolled. ¶ And now I join myself with the angels praising Him, ¶ with the dominions bowing low before Him, ¶ with the powers standing in awe. ¶ To their heavenly song of gladness I unite my own. ¶ In humble giving of thanks, I cry out: "Holy, holy, holy, Lord God of Hosts . . ." ¶ In eager expectation of Your arrival: ¶ "Blessed be He who comes . . ."

The voice of the priest is hushed, ⁋ giving an air of priestly intimacy with the miracle about to take place, ⁋ of mystery and awe before the presence of God. ⁋ The simple prayers reverently set the stage for the miracle by recalling Calvary with the sign of the cross made over the offering; ⁋ by asking God the Father to make holy the gifts to be sacrificed on the altar; ⁋ to change them into Your body and blood; ⁋ to make them a fountain of grace for the Church: ⁋ the pope, the bishop, all believers and promoters of the faith, ⁋ those especially to be remembered at this Mass; ⁋ by joining with Mary, the apostles, the saints; ⁋ by imploring God that the sacrifice be acceptable in His sight. ⁋ The priest extends his hands over our gifts. This gesture was an ancient symbol among the Jews signifying that the victim to be offered received the guilt of the offerer. ⁋ Lord Jesus, You are my victim. ⁋ You took on my guilt, the guilt of my shameful ingratitude, my neglect of duty, my willfulness, my weakness, all my sins. ⁋ For my sins You were crucified.

CONSECRATION

The great mystery of faith. ⁋ You offer Yourself again just as You did at the Last Supper and on Calvary. ⁋ Now, however, through the hands, words, and actions of Your priest, ⁋ through the offering of Your people. ⁋ Step by step the celebrant follows Your actions at the Last Supper. ⁋ In great humility of heart, he bows low and repeats the sacred words that originated on Your own sacred lips.

What was bread is now Your body. ⁋ What was wine is now Your blood.

This is the moment of transubstantiation, the changing of the substance of bread and wine into Your body and blood, while the appearances of bread and wine remain. ⁋ As the sacred body and sacred blood are raised, I adore: ⁋ "My Lord and my God!" ⁋ The gift has new value. ⁋ The gift has new meaning.

You are now before me on the altar. ¶ You present to the Father my gifts, made infinitely holy by Your coming, ¶ asking that God the Father look favorably on this offering, ¶ praying that I may also enjoy, one day, the company of the saints. ¶ The Canon ends with the minor elevation. ¶ Five times the priest forms the sign of the cross with the host. ¶ Then, taking the chalice in his left hand and the host in his right, ¶ he lifts them a few inches from the altar. ¶ "And I, if I be lifted up from the earth, will draw all things to myself."

God Accepts the Gift and Shares It

OUR FATHER

My Lord, ¶ this is Your own prayer. ¶ The Our Father joins the Consecration with the Communion. ¶ With its petition for daily food, it is a fitting prelude to Communion. ¶ In it I ask for those dispositions of charity toward God and man which are indispensable if I am to receive You worthily.

BREAKING OF THE BREAD

After a paraphrase of the last words of the Our Father, the priest breaks the host and drops a small particle of it into the chalice in imitation of what You did at the Last Supper ¶ ("Jesus took bread . . . and broke, and gave it to His disciples.") ¶ as a symbol of Your violent and bloody death on the cross.

AGNUS DEI AND PRAYERS BEFORE COMMUNION

At one time the lamb was the usual animal of sacrifice. ¶ On the cross You became my sacrificial lamb "to take away the sins of the world."

The first prayer—a prayer for peace. ¶ You come to my soul as the Prince of Peace. ¶ The soul that is calm, tranquil, free from the unrest and panicky agitation of its surroundings, is better prepared for Your coming. ¶ Lord Jesus, prepare me for Your coming, give me the gift of Your peace.

154

The second prayer—an act of faith in the Redemption, ¶ a petition for deliverance from all evils (through the merits of Your sacrifice), ¶ for all that pertains to happiness (through the reception of Your body and blood). ¶ Lord Jesus, deliver me from evil, ¶ and never allow me to be separated from You.

The third prayer—in mentioning his own unworthiness, the priest speaks for all who are to receive You. ¶ The more I know my own unworthiness the less unworthy I am to receive You. ¶ Lord Jesus, help me to prepare for Your coming.

COMMUNION

Communion is God's reward for offering a sacrifice wholly acceptable and pleasing to Him. ¶ Communion is a sacrificial banquet, a banquet of love. ¶ It is an expression of my love for You; ¶ it is an expression of my love for my fellow Christians. ¶ For You are the bond that links all Christians together. ¶ During the reception of Communion, the early Christians sang: "O Sacred Banquet, wherein Christ is received. ¶ The memory of His Passion is renewed. ¶ The mind is filled with grace, ¶ and a pledge of future glory is given to us." ¶ Lord Jesus, come into my soul!

Communion confirms and fulfills my union with You through my gifts, my offering made at the beginning of Mass. ¶ As no Communion could be had without first an offering, ¶ no offering or sacrifice can be made without a sacrificial spirit—the spirit of my life in You. ¶ I must take a sacrificial spirit to Mass. ¶ To live in the spirit of sacrifice means heroism, ¶ dedicating myself to You, ¶ accepting Your challenge to me.

PRAYERS AFTER COMMUNION

The sacrificial banquet completed, the Mass comes swiftly to an end. ¶ The remaining prayers are brief but full of meaning. ¶ They reflect the great mystery that has come to pass before the eyes of all present. ¶ The priest prays, and I by my joint action pray with him, ¶

for purity of mind, ¶ for eternal graces, ¶ for strength of soul in the face of temptation.

The Communion prayer, like the Introit and Offertory, suggests the special message of the day's Mass.

The Postcommunion, like the Collect and Secret, carries the special petition of the day, ¶ but adds the powerful reminder that now I have You within me.

Ite, missa est . . . "Go, the Mass is over." ¶ The Mass of the liturgy is ended; ¶ the Mass of life begins. ¶ Go—but first a blessing, Your blessing given through Your priest standing before the altar.

The Last Gospel is the first part of Saint John's Gospel. ¶ In the early Church this Gospel was prescribed as a prayer of thanksgiving after Mass for the priest. ¶ Later it was incorporated into the Mass itself. ¶ I say it as the first of my prayers of thanksgiving after Mass.

THANKSGIVING AFTER MASS

The minutes after I receive You are precious— ¶ You are sacramentally present with me. ¶ These minutes are rich in grace if I give You my whole attention, ¶ if I open my heart to You in words of love, adoration, thanksgiving, petition.

LIVE THE MASS

My Lord Jesus, ¶ it is the first rule of life: sharing my life with You through the Mass I sanctify myself. ¶ I share my life in presenting the works I do each day as gifts at the Offertory: ¶ my study, my job, my leisure; ¶ in uniting that offering to Yours with fervent prayer at the Consecration; ¶ in completing this union in devout Communion. ¶ You desire this offering. ¶ You pour out Your grace to me at Mass. ¶ Leaving Mass inspired by Your word and example, ¶ by Your grace, ¶ by Your presence, ¶ I can sanctify my neighbor by Your life in me.

My apostolate will be as fervent as my desire to unite with You in Mass. It can be carried on anywhere—classroom, office, factory, home.

In a Catholic life ¶ it is the Mass that matters! ¶ My Lord Jesus, with all my heart ¶ I thank You for the Mass! Amen.

Prayer before Mass

O God of love! In all humility and confidence I offer You the Immaculate Heart of Mary together with the loving Heart of Jesus our Lord, who gave Himself upon the cross of Calvary and still offers Himself upon the altar to sanctify and save the souls of men. In loving union with this sacrifice of infinite value, now being offered in *(mention the name of your country)* I offer You my whole being, O my God, and all my prayers and sufferings, all my sorrows and labors, my life and my death, in order to fulfill Your divine will in my own soul, to sanctify all missionaries and their native clergy, to obtain the grace of perseverance for their converts and the conversion of all sinners and unbelievers in their missions.

[500 days, R. 616]

Prayer of Saint Thomas Aquinas

Almighty and everlasting God, look upon me as I come to the sacrament of Your only-begotten Son, our Lord Jesus Christ. ¶ I come as one infirm to the physician of life, as one poor and needy to the Lord of heaven and earth. ¶ Therefore I implore the abundance of Your measureless bounty that You would see fit to heal my infirmity, wash my uncleanness, enlighten my blindness, enrich my poverty, and clothe my nakedness, that I may receive the Bread of Angels, the King of kings, the Lord of lords, with such reverence and humility as may be profitable to my soul's salvation. ¶ Grant me, I pray, the grace of receiving not only the sacrament of our Lord's body and blood but also the grace and power of the sacrament. ¶ O most gracious God, grant that I may so receive the body of Your only-begotten Son, our Lord Jesus Christ, which He took from the Virgin Mary, that I may deserve to be incorporated into His mystical body and to be numbered among His members. ¶ O most loving Father, give me grace to behold face to face forever Your beloved Son whom, now hidden from me in this life, I intend to receive under the sacramental veil here below. Amen.

[3 years, R. 158]

Prayers before Communion

Lord Jesus, it was a hopeless world until You came to save it. It would be a hopeless world today without Your presence in the Blessed Sacrament. Yet with You we have the fullest hope for all else. You bring us Yourself, Your strength and Your wisdom, Your knowledge of our needs and Your power to fill them. So in You I hope with complete certainty. You will do for me whatever I let You do. You will bring me all that I need. You will stay with me during my life and guide me through the gates of death into eternity. Amen.   Daniel Lord

Let the receiving of Your body, O Lord Jesus Christ, which I, though unworthy, do presume to receive, turn not to me for judgment and condemnation, but, according to Your mercy, let it be profitable to me for the receiving of protection and healing, both of soul and body: who lives and reigns for ever and ever. Amen.   [5 years, R. 155]

Prayer of Cardinal Newman

Thou comest to me at holy Mass. Let me at Holy Communion approach Thee with awe and love in whom resides all perfection and from whom I am allowed to gain it. Let me come to the Sanctifier to be sanctified. Let me come to Thee to learn my duty, and to receive grace to do it. At other times of the day I am reminded of watching, toiling, struggling, and suffering; but at this moment I am reminded simply of Thy gifts toward me a sinner.

I am reminded that I can do nothing, and that Thou dost everything. This is especially the moment of grace. I come to see and experience Thy mercies. I come before Thee as the helpless beings during Thy ministry, who were brought on beds and couches for a cure. I come to be made whole.

May each Holy Communion as it comes, find me more and more like Thee (who at these times becomest a little child for my sake) more simple-minded, more humble, more holy, more affectionate, more resigned, more happy, more full of Thee. Amen.

Cardinal Newman

Soul of Christ (Anima Christi)

Soul of Christ, sanctify me.
Body of Christ, save me.
Blood of Christ, inebriate me.
Water from the side of Christ, wash me.
Passion of Christ, strengthen me.
O good Jesus, hear me.
Within Your wounds hide me.
Permit me not to be separated from You.
From the wicked foe defend me.
At the hour of my death call me.
And bid me come to You.
That with Your saints I may praise You
For ever and ever. Amen.

[7 years, after Communion, R. 131]

Prayer before a Crucifix

Behold, O good and sweetest Jesus, I cast myself upon my knees in Your sight and with the most fervent desire of my soul I pray and beseech You to impress upon my heart lively sentiments of faith, hope, and charity, true repentance for my sins and a most firm purpose of amendment; while with deep affection and grief of soul I consider within myself and mentally contemplate Your five most precious wounds, having before my eyes that which David, the prophet, long ago spoke in Your own person concerning You, my Jesus: They have pierced my hands and my feet; they have numbered all my bones. [Plenary, usual conditions, if recited before crucifix, R. 201]

Prayer to Christ the King

O Christ Jesus, I acknowledge You to be the king of the universe; all that has been made is created for You. Exercise over me all Your sovereign rights. I hereby renew the promises of my baptism, renouncing Satan and all his works and pomps, and I engage myself to lead henceforth a truly Christian life. And in a special manner do I undertake to bring about the triumph of the rights of God and Your Church, so far as in me lies. Divine Heart of Jesus, I offer You my poor actions to obtain the acknowledgment by every heart of Your sacred kingly power. In such wise may the kingdom of Your peace be firmly established throughout all the earth.

[Plenary, usual conditions, R. 272]

Suscipe of Saint Ignatius Loyola

Receive, O Lord, all my liberty. Take my memory, my understanding, and my entire will. Whatsoever I have or hold, You have given me; I give it all back

160

to You and commit it wholly to be governed by Your will. Your love and Your grace give to me, and I am rich enough and ask for nothing more.

[3 years, R. 52]

Prayer for Generosity

Dearest Lord, teach me to be generous. Teach me to serve You as You deserve; to give and not to count the cost; to fight and not to heed the wounds; to toil and not to seek for rest; to labor and not ask for reward, save that of knowing that I am doing Your will. Amen.   Saint Ignatius Loyola

Prayer of Petition

Dear Lord, Jesus Christ, I beg that Your Passion be for me a source of strength, protection, and defense. ¶ Let Your wounds be that food and drink with which I am nourished, satisfied, and made joyous. ¶ May Your cleansing blood wash away all my sins. ¶ May Your death be my eternal life and Your cross my unending glory. ¶ In all these remembrances of Your Passion let me find new strength and exultation, vitality and happiness, God who lives and rules the world without end. Amen.

Prayer of Thanksgiving

Lord Jesus, my deep gratitude for the gift of Yourself, my thanks to You for coming to me in Communion! ¶ I adore You, the true Son of God, I want always to do Your will. ¶ After Mass I will go back to the world of men, to the work You have given me to do. ¶ But I know that You will accompany me. ¶ I will have You by my side, my companion, partner, and friend. ¶ Success or failure will be measured by my fidelity to You. ¶ Let me do well

for Your sake, and lead souls to You through my example. ¶ Consider me as one of Your close followers
in the spreading of Your kingdom on earth, as I have
united myself to You in the reception of this Holy
Communion today.

---

*For where two or three are gathered together for
my sake, there am I in the midst of them.*
Matthew 18:20

✝ *Living the Year with Christ*

Pray with Me.
Unite your prayer with Mine.
Join your prayer to the prayer of My Church,
My mystical body,
the "whole Christ."
Pray with Me,
especially in the Mass.
The Mass is part of the liturgy,
the official public prayer of the Church.
The Church prays every day of the year
    according to seasons.
This is My prayer, the prayer of My mystical body.

Knowledge of the liturgical year, its feasts
    and seasons,
is vital to you:
it enriches your mental prayer;
it aids your participation in the Mass.

The year of the liturgy is the year spent with Me.
It is no mere empty commemoration of events.

It is the sanctification of each season and all its work.
It is the year spent with Me
as I retrace the events of My life,
showing you the way to live.
This is the year spent with Mary:
her feast days show the glories of grace
and strengthen your consecration to her.
This is the year lived with the saints, My heroes,
each having a place in the calendar of the Church.

Each season of the liturgical year is meant to help
    you love Me,
to help you answer My challenge,
to help you to become more like Me.

THE LITURGICAL YEAR AND
MENTAL PRAYER

These pages can be used as helpful material for mental prayer.

For example, I ask myself: What is our Lord doing now, as with the Church I look back over His life on earth? How can I imitate Him? Apply His way of looking at things to my life?

What great truths of the faith is the Church emphasizing right now? What do they really mean to me?

What feasts of our Lady, Saint Joseph, and the other saints occur during this period? What practical application do their lives have on mine?

How is the supernatural life of the mystical body reflected in nature at this time of year? What means can I take to sanctify my activities by bringing them under the influence of the spirit of the liturgy?

Or this way: I meditate on the prayers of the Church looking through my Missal or the Breviary, using the "second method" of prayer, which is just thinking about each word and what it means, making the application to my life, integrating the mind of the Church into my own thoughts, words, and actions.

Four Sundays: First Sunday of Advent to December 24

Violet vestments are the Church's way of reminding us to prepare.

The Church's year begins:

For me: December is a month all its own . . . football ends, snow flies, days grow shorter . . . Christmas is in the air . . . thoughts of gifts . . . of going home from college, for the preparation for the holidays . . . a time of anticipation . . .

For the Church: Jesus is coming . . . the Promised One . . . coming to make a new world . . . John the Baptist preaching in the wilderness; preparing the people . . . Make straight His paths . . . the patriarchs and prophets of old longing for the Messias, the deliverer . . . Mary waits, too, in silence . . . waits for the birth of the King . . .

For both of us: A time of anticipation and preparation . . . of gift-giving and the greatest gift of all . . . from God to us . . . (for He so loved the world that He gave to us His divine Son) . . . of the joy of family love . . . and the Holy Family kneeling around the crib in perfect peace . . . with the Church I prepare for Christmas by effort and sacrifice, with Mary I wait for Jesus . . . a time of anticipation in my liturgical life: winter coming . . . home-coming . . . Christ coming . . .

Show forth Your power, O Lord, and come.

O ANTIPHONS

December 17: O Wisdom, who came out of the mouth of the Most High, reaching from end to end and ordering all things mightily and sweetly, come to teach us the way of prudence.

December 18: O Adonai and leader of the house of Israel, who did appear to Moses in the burning bush and did give him the law on Mount Sinai, come with an outstretched arm to redeem us.

December 19: O Root of Jesse, who stands as an ensign of the people, before whom kings shall keep silence and the gentiles shall make supplication, come to deliver us and tarry not.

December 20: O Key of David and scepter of the house of Israel, who opens and no man shuts, who shuts and no man opens, come and bring forth from his prison house the captive that walks in darkness and in the shadow of death.

December 21: O Dawn of the East, brightness of light eternal and Sun of Justice, come and enlighten all who sit in darkness and in the shadow of death.

December 22: O King of the Gentiles and their desired one, the cornerstone that makes both one, come and save man, whom You have made out of clay.

December 23: O Emmanuel, our King and Lawgiver, the expected one of the nations and their Redeemer, come and save us, O Lord our God.

Behold the Desired of all nations shall come, and the house of the Lord shall be filled with glory, alleluia.

Twenty Days: Christmas to January 13

White vestments are the Church's way of reminding us to rejoice.

Each day of this beautiful, wonderful season is offered in the Mass:

For me: Holidays . . . holydays . . . celebrating the day of days . . . days of celebration with family and friends . . . reunions . . . gifts and cards . . . the warm glow of colored lights and candle flame . . . red and green . . . the festive smell of mincemeat and fowl . . . that feeling of joy and peace on earth, good will to men . . . and a new year beginning . . .

For the Church: Rejoice! This day is born the Savior . . . the Word Incarnate . . . a tiny Baby in the arms of Mary . . . adored by the shepherds, the Magi, and the world . . . manifested by the martyrs Stephen, John, Thomas, the Holy Innocents . . . circumcised and called

Jesus . . . safe in the loving care of Mary and Joseph . . . the Holy Family . . . Rejoice and adore, for God is with us . . .

For both of us: Like Jesus, Mary and Joseph, our family, the Church's family, lives together, rejoices together, prays together once more united to the family circle . . . if only spiritually . . . gifts, yes . . . parties, yes . . . Mass, yes . . . gifts for the folks and friends and for Christ . . . adore Him . . . and I live my faith in the new year coming up . . . with a joyful heart to manifest the mystery of the Word made flesh . . .

The Lord said to Me: You are My Son. This day have I begotten You.

Christmas

Christ is born to us, come, let us adore.

This day shall a light shine upon us. For our sakes a Child is born, and His name shall be Peerless, God, Prince of Peace, Father of Eternity, and of His kingdom there shall be no end.

For our sakes a Child is born, to our race a Son is given, whose shoulder will bear the scepter of princely power: and His name shall be Angel of Great Counsel.

There is no corner of the world but has witnessed how our God can save.

To us is born this day a Savior. Let us rejoice. It would be unlawful to be sad today, for today is Life's birthday: the birthday of that Life which, for us dying creatures, takes away the sting of death and brings the bright promise of the eternal hereafter. It would be unlawful for any man to refuse to partake in our rejoicing. All men have an equal share in the great cause of our joy, for our Lord, who is the destroyer of sin and death, finding that all are bound under the condemnation, has come to make all free.   Pope Leo XIII

This day Christ is born, this day the Savior has appeared; this day angels are singing on earth, archangels are rejoicing; this day the just are glad and say: Glory to God in the highest, alleluia.

O wondrous exchange! the Creator of man, having assumed a living body, deigned to be born of a virgin, and having become man without man's aid, enriched us with His divinity.

Glory to God in the highest and peace on earth among men of good will, alleluia.

Epiphany

Christ has appeared among us, come, let us adore.

All the men of Saba are coming with their gifts of gold and incense, their cry of praise to the Lord. Rise up, Jerusalem, and shine forth, for the glory of the Lord has broken upon you, alleluia, alleluia. We have seen His star out in the East, and we are coming with gifts to worship the Lord, alleluia.

The precious gifts which the Magi have brought to the Lord on this day are threefold, and they are symbolical of divine mysteries: by gold the power of the King is signified, by frankincense His great priesthood, by myrrh the burial of the Lord.

Graciously look down, we beseech You, O Lord, upon the gifts of Your Church: by which gold, frankincense, and myrrh are no longer laid before You; but He is sacrificed and received who by those very gifts was signified, Jesus Christ Your Son our Lord.

The Light of light, You O Christ, have appeared; to whom the Magi bring gifts, alleluia, alleluia, alleluia.

Two—Six Weeks: January 13 to Septuagesima

Green vestments are the Church's way of reminding us to make the spirit of Christmas, the spirit of Christ, grow.

Not a letdown, but a time of challenge and growth:

For me: Holidays over . . . back to the hidden life of studies, work . . . winter passing now . . . days growing longer . . . semesters change . . . basketball begins

. . . in the fields the green winter wheat promises a rich spring harvest . . . a time of growth: intellectually, physically, spiritually . . .

For the Church: A short-path season, but important . . . commemorates the hidden life of Jesus and His public life . . . He works miracles to show His divinity . . . heals, teaches . . . invites all men to join His "New World" . . . the kingdom of Christ . . . summing up of the Christmas cycle . . . Jesus is born, grows to full manhood with Mary and Joseph and goes forth to conquer the world . . .

For both of us: With the Church I take up a hidden life with Christ at Nazareth . . . the hidden life of studies, work . . . a time of growth with Christ, I, too, prepare for my public life . . . long hours, book hours, but all Christ hours . . . the Christ at Nazareth . . . the Christ growing in wisdom and grace and age with God and men.

The works that I do in the name of My Father give testimony of Me.

Time after Epiphany

Let us pray. O Lord, we beseech You, mercifully hear the prayers of Your people who call upon You, and grant that they may both perceive what they ought to do and have grace and strength to fulfill the same, through Christ our Lord.

Let us pray. Grant to us, O Lord, we beseech You, the spirit to think and do always such things as are right, that we who cannot exist without You may be able to live according to Your will, through our Lord.

Let us adore the Lord, for He Himself has made us.

Benediction and glory and wisdom and thanksgiving, honor and power and strength to our God for ever and ever. Amen.

The Lord is King; He has clothed Himself in majesty.

The Lord has clothed and girded Himself with power.

God is love, and he who abides in love abides in God and God in him.

*Septuagesima: Septuagesima Sunday to
Holy Saturday*
Violet vestments remind us to prepare.
Lent: the forty days from Ash Wednesday to Holy
Saturday.
Passiontide: the last two weeks of Lent, Passion Week
and Holy Week.

Winter changes to spring, and brings:
For me: March winds and a fresh clean smell . . .
spring plowing . . . planting the seeds in yard and garden
. . . out comes the baseball mitt to prepare for spring
training . . . house cleaning . . . clean-up, paint-up, light-
up working together . . . a time of renovation . . . a
time of rebirth . . .
For the Church: Easter cycle begins . . . a transition,
a new focus: the Redemption of fallen man by the new
Adam, Jesus Christ . . . foreshadowed by the Old Testament leaders . . . Jesus begins His mission . . . forty
days in the desert, fasting, preparing . . . then His
preaching and teaching . . . but His own received Him
not . . . (for unless the seed die) . . . He offers Himself
as our victim . . . undergoing a shameful death . . . even
the death of the cross . . . to win for us new life . . .
For both of us: With Christ I prepare manfully for
the struggle against sin . . . Lent: like a long retreat
ending with Easter . . . with Christ I fast, do penance,
train spiritually . . . cleaning house in my spiritual life
. . . then self-offering to Him . . . obedience and generosity . . . serving others for Him . . . to repay . . . no
man ever had greater love . . . for me . . . than this . . .
Son of Man, the King of Glory upon the cross . . .
*Behold: by the wood of the cross joy came into the
whole world.*

Lent
Be converted to Me with all your heart in fasting, in
weeping, and in mourning. And rend your hearts, not
your garments, says the Lord God almighty.

O God, You see that we have no power whatever from ourselves. Keep us both outwardly in our bodies and inwardly in our souls that we may be defended from all adversities which may happen to the body and from all evil thoughts which may hurt the soul.

This time of fasting has opened to us the gates of paradise; let us accept it, praying that on the day of resurrection we may be glorified securely in the Lord.

With the armor of justice let us give ourselves to much patience and fasting.

Passiontide

As we gaze upon Him, no stateliness here, no majesty, no beauty! Our sins, and it was He who bore them, He who suffered for us. It was for our wickedness He was wounded, by His bruises we were healed. Our weakness, and it was He who carried the weight of it, our miseries, and it was He who bore them.

God did not spare even His own Son, but gave Him up for us all.

My people, what have I done to you? or in what have I grieved you? Answer Me. I brought you out of Egypt having drowned Pharao in the Red Sea: and you have delivered Me to the chief priests. I opened the sea before you: and you with a spear have opened My side. I gave you the water of salvation from the rock to drink: and you have given Me gall and vinegar. My people, what have I done to you, or in what have I grieved you? Answer Me. Lefebvre

Eight Weeks: Easter to Trinity Sunday

White vestments mark the celebration of Paschaltide.

Spring brings new vigor and new life:

For me: Spring days . . . sunny days . . . nature bursting forth in buds and blossoms . . . April showers and May flowers . . . holidays . . . flowers for my mother or the best girl . . . double-headers and walks in the park . . . a time of freshness and life . . .

170

For the Church: Christ risen! Victory . . . Alleluia . . . high point of the year . . . Christ our Pasch is sacrificed . . . Jesus conquers death and merits the grace of our supernatural life . . . May, Mary's month . . . reunited with her Son . . . then the Ascension . . . Jesus goes to prepare a place and send His Spirit . . . a mighty wind, tongues of fire . . . minds enlightened . . . hearts warmed . . . wills strengthened, the apostles become real men . . . full of vigor, determination . . . the Holy Spirit takes possession of His Church . . .

For both of us: With Christ I rise and walk in the way of grace . . . happy because He is happy . . . sharing the victory over the old ways . . . pledging my loyalty, I renew my baptismal promises . . . through Mary's help I put new vigor into my spiritual life . . . waiting like the apostles for the Spirit to make me a man of courage . . . a modern apostle . . .

I arose and am still with you, alleluia!

Easter

The Lord is truly risen, alleluia.

This is the day the Lord has made! Let us rejoice and be glad therein!

If you have risen with Christ, seek the things that are above, where Christ is seated at the right hand of God. Mind the things that are above, not the things that are on earth.

His countenance was like lightning and His raiment like snow, alleluia, alleluia.

Easter! The Easter of the Lord! And again may I say it: it is Easter! that I may honor the most Blessed Trinity. Today is the feast of feasts, the solemnity of solemnities; it surpasses not only those that are secular and worldly in character, but even excels, as the sun outshines all stars, those feasts which are dedicated to and are celebrated in honor of Christ Himself.

Saint Gregory of Nazianzen

I ascend to My Father and to your Father, to My God and your God, alleluia.

171

Pentecost

Alleluia, the Spirit of the Lord has filled the whole world; come, let us adore.

The Spirit of the Lord fills the whole world, alleluia. The whole frame of created things recognizes the accents of His voice, alleluia.

May our hearts be cleansed by the inpouring of Your Holy Spirit, Lord, and may our souls grow fertile under the dew He sheds upon them.

Twenty-three—Twenty-eight Weeks: Trinity Sunday to Advent

Green vestments symbolize the growth of the Church under the reign of the Holy Spirit.

Every day of summer and autumn has its own particular importance:

For me: Summer days . . . billowing clouds and glorious skies . . . vacations . . . warm sun and cool water . . . the soft evening air at a dance . . . June brides . . . a summer job . . . fields of ripening grain . . . the splash of autumn color . . . the World Series, football . . . then school . . . harvest time . . . Thanksgiving . . . a time of fulfillment . . .

For the Church: The Church's summer and autumn . . . the extension of the reign of the Holy Spirit begun at Pentecost . . . continuing the work of Christ . . . the Church celebrates the great mysteries of the faith: the Holy Trinity . . . the Blessed Sacrament . . . the love of the Sacred Heart . . . Mary's assumption into heaven . . . the rosary . . . Christ the King . . . the communion of saints . . . a time of fulfillment . . . the Holy Spirit overshadows the world and a rejoicing Church celebrates with her people . . .

For both of us: The fasts of Lent and the spring of Easter now burst forth in the full fruit and flower of Pentecost . . . I take my place in the Church . . . the mystical body . . . nourished by the Bread of Life, I grow in grace . . . produce a harvest of good works . . .

and under Mary's protection . . . hope to join the ranks of the saints . . . the real fulfillment of my life . . .

Send forth Your Spirit . . . and You shall renew the face of the earth.

Time after Pentecost

His kingdom is an everlasting kingdom, and all kings shall serve Him and shall obey Him.

Brethren: we joyfully render thanks to the Father, who has made us worthy to share the lot of the saints in light. He has rescued us from the power of darkness and transferred us into the kingdom of His beloved Son.

The First-born of the dead, and the Ruler of the kings of the earth has made us a kingdom to God and His Father, alleluia.

His empire shall be multiplied.
And there shall be no end of peace.

Rise and pray, . . .
Luke 22:46

Prayer

☦

You have not chosen Me but I have chosen you.
I chose to create you,
to give you the life of grace,
to give you every blessing.
To show you that I really care for you,
that I love you with an eternal love,
I died on the cross.
Greater love than this no one has,
that one lay down his life for his friends.

173

Do not wonder, then, that I am interested
in everything you do,
in every thought you think,
in every breath you breathe.
I want you to be secure, extremely happy, at peace.
That peace of soul which I had on earth
I left to you.
I gave it to you
not as the world gives its peace,
a mere respite between sufferings,
but I left you a peace so profound
that neither the world nor anything else
can ever rob you of it.
This peace of soul is your closeness to Me.

We come ever closer together by our intimate talks.
You tell Me your fears, worries, heartaches,
your joys, hopes, plans for the future.
I listen to every word,
for whatever happens to you
happens to Me,
and whatever anyone does to you in the least way
he does to Me.
This is how close we are.
You confide in Me and I confide in you.
This is prayer.

The world is sick,
dying from its own brutal, willful sins.
I am distressed
to see so many of My own on the road to hell.
These poor vagabonds are Mine,
who really want My love
but have let themselves be blinded by Satan.
Someone must save them.
Someone must shield these little ones of mine.

I have chosen you to do this work with Me,
for Me,
in Me.

This then is My challenge to you:
if you love Me,
if you choose to help others,
then be a man who can talk to his God,
be a man of prayer.

What Is Prayer?

Prayer is the lifting of the mind and heart to God for the purpose of adoring Him (adoration), ¶ thanking Him (thanksgiving), ¶ asking for His forgiveness (satisfaction), ¶ begging of His goodness (petition). ¶ Prayer is a human act because it is said with full knowledge, ¶ full deliberation, ¶ full consent. ¶ When these three marks are present, the act is a human act. ¶ It is creditable to a human being as being his or her own. ¶ Hence, when I pray with the above three marks present, the prayer is truly "mine" even though I did not write it. ¶ By "lifting up the mind" we think about God, ¶ we understand His eternal truths, ¶ we ponder His words and their meaning. ¶ Our prayer then is intelligent and not sheer emotion. ¶ But we do employ our emotions, too. ¶ The emotions are driving forces which help the will to its end. ¶ But the will freely chooses. ¶ Our prayer is then a free act. ¶ This free act, freely dedicated to God, is one of man's most pleasing gifts to his Creator.

Need of Prayer

Prayer is necessary to salvation, and without it no one who must live and battle in the world can be saved. ¶ Prayer keeps us close to our Blessed Lord, which means we share more in the Christ-life, ¶ the life of grace, both sanctifying and actual. ¶ Prayer keeps us from sin, ¶ protects us from temptations, ¶ brings our desires in tune

175

with God's, ¶ gives us power to help our fellow man, ¶ makes martyrs, saints, virgins, and confessors, ¶ brings us finally face to face with God.

Our Lord has said to us: Ask and it shall be given to you, ¶ seek and you shall find, ¶ knock and it shall be opened to you. ¶ For everyone who asks receives, ¶ and he who seeks finds, ¶ and to him who knocks it shall be opened.

Need of Mental Prayer

The true Christian must not only talk to God in his prayer, but he must often think of God. ¶ Mary is our example. ¶ Mary contemplated Jesus, ¶ she pondered His every word. ¶ When Jesus returned to Nazareth after being lost in the Temple, "His Mother kept all these things carefully in her heart." ¶ After the shepherds made their visit, "Mary kept in mind all their words, pondering them in her heart." ¶ Immediately after the Ascension "All these with one mind continued steadfastly in prayer with the women and Mary, the Mother of Jesus, and with His brethren."

Saint Paul realized the importance of mental prayer when he wrote to Timothy: "Meditate on these things, give yourself entirely to them that your progress may be manifest to all."

Things of sense—what I see, taste, hear, touch, and smell make an immediate appeal to me. ¶ I am directly, immediately, and automatically attracted to them. ¶ But I must also be attracted to the higher values in life. ¶ I must be patriotic, honest, pure, charitable, and apostolic. ¶ But I cannot feel or touch or see the values of these virtues. ¶ Virtue must enter my mind to attract me. ¶ The words of our Lord must bury themselves deep in my thoughts where they will be always with me, where they will inspire me to live the Christ-life. ¶ I cannot see Christ but I can know His warm love. ¶ I cannot hear Christ but I can treasure His words. ¶ I cannot touch Christ but I can become so much like Him as to be one with Him. ¶ I can do all these by mental prayer.

Mental prayer saturates me with the Christ-mind. ¶ Now not I but Christ lives in me. ¶ I think Christ's way, ¶ I judge Christ's way, ¶ I feel Christ's way, ¶ I love Christ's way. ¶ By mental prayer, Christ whispers to me His every wish. ¶ I become a fortress against Satan's attacks. ¶ I begin to "put on Christ," to become another Christ. ¶ I draw closer to my Lord. ¶ I fill my mind so much with Christ that it is almost psychologically impossible to sin.

Ease of Prayer

How easy it is to pray! ¶ When we look at the distant horizon and follow the sun setting in all its brilliance, trailed by a radiant glow of color— ¶ how easy it is to bless God for His creation.

How easy to thank God when our hearts are full of joy! ¶ When our Blessed Mother visited Elizabeth, her heart was overflowing with gladness. ¶ She was anxious to tell someone of her great happiness. ¶ She had just received the body of Christ. ¶ It was like making her first Holy Communion. ¶ Mary's prayer on this occasion is one of the most beautiful ever uttered by human lips, and yet it is not strained, not mechanical. ¶ Mary was full of joy that God was with her, and from the depths of her heart there arose that song of jubilee which swelled till it could no longer be contained. ¶ It burst forth into the beautiful Magnificat.

The Magnificat

My soul magnifies the Lord, and my spirit rejoices in God my Savior; ¶ because He has regarded the lowliness of His handmaid; ¶ for, behold, henceforth all generations shall call me blessed; ¶ because He who is mighty has done great things for me, and holy is His name; ¶ and for generation upon generation is His mercy, to those who fear Him. ¶ He has shown might with His arm, ¶ He has scattered the proud in the conceit of their heart. ¶ He has put down the mighty from their thrones, ¶ and has exalted the lowly. ¶ He has filled the hungry with good things, ¶ and the rich He has sent away empty. ¶ He has given help to Israel, His servant, mindful of His mercy— ¶ even as He spoke to our father—to Abraham and to his posterity forever.

[3 years, R. 320]

At times, the soul may express a prayer in a simple word. ¶ Mary Magdalene was heartbroken when she found her Lord had been taken from the tomb. ¶ She sat in tears. ¶ Then, suddenly, He appeared, ¶ and with all the love that had taken her from the ways of sin to the ways of sanctity, she exclaimed: Rabboni! ¶ Our Blessed Mother must have prayed with only one word when her Son appeared to her after Calvary: one word was enough—Jesus!

God is interested in everything we have to say. ¶ That is why prayer is so easy. ¶ We must talk to God in our own individual way. ¶ My way of prayer will be my very own. ¶ There are norms and rules which I must follow that my prayer will be proper. ¶ But I will express my thoughts, my feelings, in my own way. ¶ The great saints of God had the same heroic aspirations and thoughts, but they expressed themselves differently. ¶ All the saints loved God in a heroic manner, but all told God of their love in their own individual way. ¶ Listen to the saints!

Job

The devil asked permission of God to tempt Job because God had boasted of Job: "There is none like him in the earth, a simple and upright man, and fearing God, and avoiding evil." After the devil robbed Job of all his possessions, Job prayed:

Naked came I out of my mother's womb, and naked shall I return there: the Lord gave, and the Lord has taken away; as it has pleased the Lord so is it done. Blessed be the name of the Lord.

Job 1:8-21

David

O Lord, how many are my adversaries, many rise up against me!

There are many who say of me: "There is no help for him in God."

But you, O Lord are my shield, my glory, the one who lifts up my head.

With a loud voice I cried unto the Lord, and he answered me from his holy mountain.

I lay down and slept: I arose for the Lord upholds me.

I shall not fear even thousands of people, arrayed against me on every side.

Arise, O Lord! Save me, my God! For you have struck all my enemies on the jaw, you have broken the teeth of the wicked.

Salvation is of the Lord: your blessing be upon your people.   Psalm 3

Prayer of Petition

O Lord my God, be attentive to my prayer. Let Your mercy grant my desire, since it does not burn for myself alone, but longs to serve the charity I have for my brethren; and in my heart You see that it is so. Let me offer in sacrifice to You the service of my mind and my tongue, and do You give me what I may offer to You. For I am needy and poor, You are rich to all who call upon You. You are free from care for Yourself and full of care for us. Circumcise the lips of my mouth and the lips of my mind of all rash speech and lying. May Your Scriptures be for my chaste delight; let me not deceive others about them nor be myself deceived. O Lord, hearken and have mercy, O Lord my God, light of the blind, and strength of the weak, but light too of the clear of sight and strength of the strong; hearken to my soul, hear it crying from the depths. Unless Your ears are attentive to us in the abyss, whither shall we go? To whom shall we cry?   Saint Augustine

Prayer for Forgiveness
Lord Jesus Christ, who did stretch out Your hands on the cross, and redeem us by Your blood. Forgive me, a sinner, for none of my thoughts are hidden from You. Pardon I ask, pardon I hope for, pardon I trust to have. You who are pitiful and merciful, spare me, and forgive.   Saint Ambrose

Prayer for Mercy
Show me, O Lord, Your mercy, and delight my heart with it. ¶ Let me find You, whom so longingly I seek.

See. Here is the man whom the robbers seized and mishandled, and left half-dead on the road to Jericho. ¶ You who can do what the kindhearted Samaritan cannot do; come to my aid!

I am the sheep who wandered into the wilderness; seek after me, and bring me home to Your fold. ¶ Do with me whatever You will, that all the days of my life I may bide by You, and praise You, with all those who are in heaven with You for all eternity. Amen.   Saint Jerome

Prayer for God's Protection

May the strength of God pilot us. ¶ May the power of God preserve us. ¶ May the wisdom of God instruct us. ¶ May the hand of God protect us. ¶ May the way of God direct us. ¶ May the shield of God defend us. ¶ May the host of God guard us—against the snares of the evil ones,—against temptations of the world. Amen.   Saint Patrick

Prayer for Love of God

Grant, O Lord, that the sweet violence of Your most ardent love may disengage and separate me from everything that is under heaven, and entirely consume me, that I may die for the love of Your infinite love. This I beg of You, O Son of God, who died for love of me. My God and my all! Who are You, O sweetest Lord! and who am I?—Your servant and a base worm. I desire to love You, most holy Lord. I have consecrated my soul to You, and my body, with all that I am. If I knew what to do more perfectly to glorify You, this I would do most ardently. Yes, this I most ardently desire to accomplish, O my God. Amen.   Saint Francis of Assisi

Prayer for Suffering

O Son of the eternal Father, Jesus Christ, our Lord and King of all, what have You left behind You in the world that, as Your heirs, we could inherit from You? What have You possessed but sorrow, pain, but ignominy and a tree, on which You were to suffer a most bitter death? O God, we, Your true children, who will not abandon our inheritance, shall not flee from suffering. Amen.

Saint Teresa of Avila

Prayer for Detachment

Lord, grant that, indifferent to all that is not commanded by You, indifferent to all those creatures the use of which You have not even forbidden, my heart may neither desire nor seek, among the multiplicity of creatures and the vicissitudes of life, anything except what is needed for the fulfillment of Your will. May health or sickness, riches or poverty, honors or contempt, humiliations, leave my soul, if not insensible, at least in that state of holy indifference to which I desire to attain for Your greater honor and greater glory. For this I pray. Amen.

Saint Ignatius Loyola

Prayer to the Divine Face

O Jesus, who in Your cruel Passion did become the reproach of men, the Man of Sorrows, I worship Your divine face. Once it shone with the beauty and sweetness of Your divinity; now for my sake it has become as the face of a leper. Yet in that disfigured countenance I recognize Your infinite love and I am consumed with the desire of loving You and of making You loved by all mankind. The tears that streamed in such abundance from Your eyes are to me as precious pearls, which I delight to gather, that with their infinite worth may be ransomed the souls of poor sinners. O Jesus, whose face is the sole beauty that ravishes my heart! The sweetness of Your glance here upon earth I may not behold, to this I consent, but I pray You to imprint in me Your divine likeness. With Your love, I implore You, so inflame me that it may quickly consume me, as soon as I may reach in heaven the vision of Your glorious face. Amen.

Saint Thérèse of Lisieux

Readiness for Prayer

The first thing we must do to prepare ourselves for converse with God is to live according to His wishes. Keeping the commandments, practicing acts of charity, humility, obedience, chastity, and so on, prepare us to talk to God in prayer. If we are faithful to our daily obligations, we will always be ready for prayer.

The State of Prayer (Recollection)

When we are in a state of mental nearness to God, we instinctively think of Him, of His wishes, of His love, of His laws. This state of mind is called "recollection." It is not acquired directly but is rather the result and outcome of our actual prayers, of our attendance at Mass and Benediction, of the sermons we hear and of the spiritual books we read. We can help our recollection especially by frequent ejaculations and visits to the Blessed Sacrament.

This state of mind, whereby we feel very close to our Blessed Lord, shall not give us a long face. On the contrary, we realize we are close to the one we love above all others, and that He wants us to be close to Him. This state of soul is the precious pearl all men seek, but for which so few know where to look.

Actual, or explicit, prayer is an actual lifting of the mind and heart to God for the purpose of adoring Him, thanking Him, asking His forgiveness, and begging of His goodness. We begin our actual prayer by recalling to whom we are going to speak—by making an act of the presence of God.

The Act of Recalling the Presence of God

A good coach usually gathers his team together before the big game to make sure they all realize exactly what they are about to do. If the players have been distracted by their trip or by an exam, they have to collect their wits and realize that the main task here and now is to win this game. Before one visits a prelate or some person of renown, he first tries to put himself into the right frame of mind. Everything must be proper and apropos. The same is true for prayer. Before we pray we must realize to whom we intend to address ourselves. The "last-minute touch" before prayer we call the "act of recollection" because, though we realize we are always in God's presence, at the time for prayer we want to be especially conscious of our Lord's nearness. Before Mass the priest and altar boys say some prayers at the foot of the altar just to remind themselves of the eternal sacrifice about to be offered.

We can vary the process greatly, for instance: in Advent we think of God as the "one about to come"; in Lent we recall some aspect of our Lord's Passion; in Eastertide we re-create some aspect of His risen life; the time required for a good act of recollection may vary greatly. It may take us a very short while or we may spend the whole time of prayer thinking about God's presence. The only rule as regards the act of recollection is that rule of Saint Ignatius, which should be applied to all the phases of prayer, namely: so long as one is gaining from the present consideration, that is, so long as a deeper insight, appreciation, or satisfaction is being gained from the present point being considered, remain meditating on this point. Move to the next point only when the present one has been exhausted.

But remember! The act of recollection reminds us of the closeness of our Blessed Lord. When we realize how close He is to us and how attentive to what we say, we will pray openly, eagerly, and with confidence, revealing to our Lord all we have to tell. The act of recollection then is very important because it can set the tone of our whole prayer.

Vocal Prayer

"I have cried to the Lord with my voice. . . . O Lord, open my lips, and my mouth shall declare Your praise."

Vocal prayers are patterns of ideas, set to formulas of words. We recite the words expressing the ideas as our

184

own. This is a perfectly good way to pray. Our Lord Himself said: When you pray say:

> Our Father,
> who art in heaven
> hallowed be Thy name.
> Thy kingdom come, Thy will be done
> on earth as it is in heaven.
> Give us this day our daily bread.
> And forgive us our trespasses
> as we forgive those who trespass against us.
> And lead us not into temptation
> but deliver us from evil.
> Amen.

Many times we will not be able to pray for a long period, but we will want to talk to God anyway. Vocal prayer is one way to keep our "contact" with God during the busy times of the day. Aspirations, short vocal prayers, are easily memorized and can be recited throughout the day no matter how busy we are. Father LeBuffe tells the story of a traffic cop who carried his beads in his pocket and would say them during "off moments." Since the words and phrases are not new and do not come fresh from our minds, we can easily be distracted. What to do?

First, we can concentrate on the enunciation and the pronunciation of the words. When first brought before a person of rank we are careful lest we enunciate sloppily and make a poor impression. The same is true when talking with our Lord. But just as it would be unnatural to keep conscious of the pronunciation for long periods of time, we should not continue at this for too long a time at prayer. We can also think of the meaning of the words. Each word adds something to the prayer. Hail Mary . . . Mother . . . of God . . . But here too we cannot follow this method too long.

Perhaps the best way to keep recollected during vocal prayer is to center our thoughts on God the Father, our Blessed Lord, our Blessed Mother, one of the saints, a particular mystery of the rosary, and so on. Or perhaps we will want to thank God for some grace He has given us. We can then pray with the idea of thanking Him. Then we will sincerely mean what we say and our prayer will be a devout one. To attain the Dominican indulgence on the rosary, however, one must meditate on the mystery of the rosary. Though we can think of God under some aspect while we pray, in order to gain the indulgence, the prayers must be said without any additions, omissions, or changes in the words.

Remember that God will grant us special graces to pray well. Hence, we should feel very much at home at prayer, for with the right intention and with the desire to show God our love for Him and our need of Him, we can pray with confidence for we know our prayer will be accepted by Him.

Public Vocal Prayer

From time to time Catholics can pray together. "That with one mind and with one mouth, you may glorify God and the Father of our Lord, Jesus Christ." Praying aloud together is like a battalion on review. The Catholics raise their voices in praise of God, kneeling shoulder to shoulder, at attention before the King. When they band together to pray they are offering public worship, binding themselves together in a closer union with our Lord and giving good example both to each other and to outsiders who may witness their devotion.

Mental Prayer

This type of prayer is the lifting of the mind and heart to God by means of thought.

It is thinking about the things of God, in the presence of God, and applying them to ourselves. Everyone likes to mull things over in his mind: we think about a social event, a very close friend, our vocation in life. Now whenever we mull over the things of God we are actually praying mentally.

"I will pray with the spirit, I will pray also with the understanding."

We think about the things of God—in the presence of God. In prayer, we are talking to God and since this is a real conversation, two at least must participate. God is really listening to me and wanting very much to tell me many things. But because I cannot see Him nor hear His voice like the first apostles could, I must continually recall mentally that our Lord is as present to me as He was to the first apostles on the shores of Galilee. If I am a genuine Christian, one dedicated to the service of Jesus Christ, then I will sincerely strive to make my love of God affect my whole life. In other words, I am practical in my love of God, applying our Lord's principles to my own life. Christ is the model. I imitate Him by applying His principles and His values to my life.

Hence, we can see the great value of mental prayer. We take on the mind of Jesus Christ so that now, not I, but Christ lives in me.

METHODS OF MENTAL PRAYER

Meditation

By "meditation" we mean thinking about some general principle, some general truth of the spiritual life, in the presence of God, and applying it to ourselves making it personal and, therefore, meaningful. Thus we meditate on the end of man, on sin, on death, on hell. Let us take for an example a short meditation on the words of Jesus, "What shall it profit a man if he gain the whole world and suffer the loss of his own soul?"

Contemplation

By "contemplation" we mean re-enacting a scene from the life of our Lord, our Blessed Mother, or the saints. *Contemplare* is the Latin verb meaning "to look at," so we take a just-as-though-I-were-present attitude. We put ourselves on the scene and take part in it ourselves. It is like going to the movies and seeing ourselves in a scene with our Lord. Books on the life of our Lord, on the Holy Land, will give us a full source of abundant material to vitalize our contemplations. Through contemplation today's Christian becomes accustomed to being with our Lord and conversing with Him.

The Three Methods of Prayer of Saint Ignatius

At the conclusion of the *Spiritual Exercises,* Saint Ignatius adds three other ways of praying. We must remember that any "method" or "way" of prayer must be used by us only to the extent it attains our purpose, which is to come closer to our Blessed Lord. If the method is good for us, we should use it to advantage. But what will help one will not necessarily help another. Hence, we apply the principle *tantum-quantum.*

The *tantum-quantum* principle of Saint Ignatius means we use a thing only inasmuch as and to the extent that it helps us. But insofar as it hinders us, we avoid it. Spiritual direction will often be needed to help us know whether we are praying correctly or not.

At times we feel that our prayer is a thorough failure. We do not seem to be getting a deeper appreciation of a fundamental truth or filling our minds with thoughts of God or drawing closer to our Lord. Yet, provided we have a good intention and have properly prepared ourselves for prayer, provided we give the full time to prayer and we observe the proper form or manner of prayer, in short, provided we do what we can, then, our prayer is an excellent one. One great lesson of prayer we must learn is this: We must always try to do our best but the results we leave up to God. If God sends us special "lights" (insights) or graces or comforting thoughts or inspirations or resolutions, we must be especially grateful, but our job is to offer God our efforts, to pray as well as we can, to trust that God will grant us graces according to His infinite wisdom and love.

In other words, if we do everything we are supposed to by way of effort, then we can truly say that every such prayer we offer is an excellent one. To realize how much God values our poor efforts is to begin to realize His tremendous love for us and how utterly confident we should be under His loving protection.

188

First Method of Prayer

This method is to reflect on the commandments of God or the Church, the seven capital sins, the virtues we particularly need, the talents God has given us and what He expects from them. We consider the importance of the commandment, the rule, the virtue, how it will make us more Christlike, its holiness, obligation, usefulness, practicality, how we have observed it in a general way, how we should observe it in the future. In other words, it is an extended and prayerful general examination of conscience.

Second Method of Prayer

This method is to take any vocal prayer and meditate on the individual words and phrases of it. We dwell on a particular word so long as we have something to think about, or something which merits our attention. Sometimes a whole meditation can be spent dwelling on the words "Our Father."

Saint Ignatius writes: The second method of prayer is that the person, kneeling or seated, according to the greater disposition in which he finds himself and as more devotion accompanies him, keeping the eyes closed or fixed on one place, without moving them about, says "Father" and continues to think over this word so long as he finds meaning, comparisons, relish, and consolation in considerations pertaining to this word. And let him act in the same way with each word of the Our Father, or of any prayer which he wants to say in this way.

To put this briefly and in outline:

1 Stay on a word or phrase so long as I find anything to think about. Only then, pass on to the next word or phrase.
2 Finish off the rest of the prayer vocally.
3 Short colloquy to the person to whom the vocal prayer is addressed. This should always end the period of mental prayer; and we should freely chat during the whole period of prayer much in the same way as we would talk with a close friend.

4 Begin the next day by reciting the prayer vocally up to the word or phrase upon which I had been meditating earlier.

5 Any vocal prayer can be meditated upon thus: Hail Mary, Creed, Confiteor, Mass prayers, or litanies.

Third Method of Prayer

This method is like the second method, with this addition, that we reflect on a different word with every breath we take. It is a "breath-by-breath" meditation. Saint Ignatius calls it a "prayer of rhythm." He writes: "The Third Method of Prayer is that with each breath or with each respiration one prays mentally, saying one word of the Our Father, or of another prayer which one recites, so that only one word is said between one breath to another, and in the length of time between each breath, attention should be paid chiefly to the meaning of the word in question or to the person to whom the prayer is said, or to his own baseness, or to the difference between such greatness and his own smallness. And in the same form and manner he will proceed in the other words of the Our Father, and the other prayers."

This method is very helpful when we are tired, for the rhythm helps keep us alert and active in our prayer. As in the case of other types of prayer, some will find it helpful, and some will find little fruit in using it. We must be guided by our spiritual father and by our own experience. No example, of course, can be given of this method of prayer.

Meditative Reading

Mental prayer is difficult for beginners because they do not feel at home with it, they do not have many thoughts on which to dwell, many ideas to sustain their prayer. Spiritual reading can fill the mind with thoughts, with insights and reflections, which will provide an abundant source of material that can be used in our prayer. Read over a good spiritual book slowly, meditatively. You will be surprised how much you get out of it. The book should be a good spiritual book, one suited for you, for your state of soul at the present time, for your state in life, for your age. Your spiritual father will be your best guide here—consult him on your reading.

Colloquy

A colloquy is an intimate and reverent chat with our Lord. We can make colloquies throughout our prayer, as the inspiration of the Holy Spirit will direct us. We should end the mental prayer by talking over the matter of our prayer, telling our Lord how it affected us, how we feel about it, and asking graces for the future.

If we feel highly encouraged after prayer, we tell our Lord so. If we feel the ideals are too lofty, we tell our Lord so and ask for His grace. In brief, we tell God exactly how we feel after meditating, in a simple child-like way.

Resolutions

If we love our Lord we will want to be like Him. A good Catholic will sincerely want to root out the many faults he has and take on the wonderful virtues of our Lord. So he resolves to be better.

But we cannot let ourselves be content with such vague resolutions as "to be more Christlike," "to be better parishioners." We must hit ourselves harder than that. We must be more definite, more specific.

If my charity is not the charity of a perfect Christian, then perhaps I should resolve: not to lose my temper when X pushes into me, not to judge X when he makes a catty remark.

If my humility is not that which is required of a follower of the humble Christ, then perhaps I should resolve: to do my best in school and work so that I may use the talents God gave me not merely to do better than X, but also to try not to feel jealous of the attention X receives.

Every prayer need not contain such specific resolutions. Sometimes we will want to take refuge in God during prayer, to fill our minds with thoughts of Him. This is sufficient. If we meditate well, resolutions will follow naturally.

In mental prayer we develop a mental attitude, a desire for God, a hierarchy of values, an apostolic frame of mind. This is how our minds become more like Christ's. Our wills are then drawn naturally to follow the standards the mind accepts.

Hence, we are becoming more and more like Christ simply by praying well.

Pray Always!

Our Lord tells us we must pray always. But because of the many duties of our state of life we cannot always be making acts of prayer. By making the Morning Offering we dedicate all our acts of the day to God: everything we do becomes a prayer. The motto of the Benedictines is "to labor is to pray." Saint Ignatius writes: "We should look for the presence of God in all things, in our conversations, in our walks, when we are using our eyes, listening or thinking, when we are eating, and in all that we do."

The genuine Christian fills his day with Mass, mental prayer, with examen, and the rosary. The "off moments" can be filled with ejaculations, brief periods of mental prayer, some favorite vocal prayers. If all these duties are performed well, we will soon have the spirit of recollection so that despite the busy life we lead we can easily and frequently turn our thoughts to God. Hence, our day can be refreshed with intermittent prayer.

Archbishop Goodier sums up, in the following way, the spirit of praying always:

Conscious—not only in words, but thoughts flashed across the mind: aspirations in the midst of our actions, acts of purity of intention, passive conformity to God's will, active conformity to God's will, imitation of Christ in a particular action, recollection of God's presence.

Subconscious—a spontaneous act resulting from a habit: aspirations rather spontaneously and effortlessly made, faithful cooperation with grace and with the inspirations of the Holy Spirit.

Unconscious—an instinct to turn to God in everything. Such souls instinctively see the hand of God in trials, sufferings, graces, favors, and so on. Aspirations such as "Thy will be done" or "Blessed be the will of God" come to the lips instinctively.

Progress in Mental Prayer

From the daily practice of mental prayer the individual will soon notice a growing familiarity and facility. This progress will usually appear over longer spans of time; it will not, ordinarily, be noticeable from day to day. Periods of dryness, that is, periods when prayer seems especially difficult (for some reason or other), will be experienced from time to time. God may use this "dryness" as a period of trial to prepare us for greater graces or merely to "sharpen" our love and service of Him. The spiritual father will aid greatly in searching for the causes of this dryness.

In general, the sincere person will make real progress in mental prayer. Each soul will be tutored individually by our Blessed Lord, but we shall lay down some general indications of progress in mental prayer.

In the beginning, we must develop solid and deep convictions of the truths of the spiritual life. Hence, we must use our mind more than our will: reasoning, reflecting, analyzing, applying our principles to our own life.

Then we must sincerely and thoroughly desire these truths and principles. Hence, we begin what is called "affective" prayer; we increase our will-activity: sorrow for sin, thanksgiving, joy, petition, love.

Next, these affections become less varied, more simple, and protracted. Hence, we begin to live more or less habitually in the presence of God: a simple and affectionate gaze upon God, a remembrance of God, a tendency toward God.

Finally, there is mystical prayer which is a tremendous grace for which we may humbly pray. But it is beyond the scope of our treatment to handle mystical prayer here.

Choosing a Spiritual Father

Most people need the guidance and expert advice of a spiritual director if they hope to persevere and make progress in their prayer and strivings after Christian virtue. The very title "spiritual father" indicates the intimate relationship between the priest and the Christian. Pope Leo XIII wrote (to Cardinal Gibbons on *Americanism*): "God in His infinite providence has decreed that men, for the most part, should be saved by men; hence, He has appointed that those whom He calls to a loftier degree of holiness should be led thereto by men."

Even professional men consider the guidance they receive from their advisers of the utmost importance. We are seldom good judges in our own case. We either ignore tepidity or conjure up scruples; but seldom can we find for ourselves the middle ground of perfection. A spiritual father, to whom our soul is freely open, can take an objective look without any emotional bias. From him the Catholic can learn norms so that he will be able to handle the ordinary spiritual problems on his own.

It may be some time before a person finds a priest to whom he can be completely open. He should not "leap before he looks." But God will surely provide the suitable guide in due time. He can practice humility and obedience by following the directions of his spiritual father.

What should the spiritual father know? Anything and everything we feel he should know: our spiritual life, ¶ our present habitual sins and imperfections, ¶ our bad inclinations and inordinate affections, ¶ those past sins which still affect our present state of soul, ¶ our virtues, ¶ our progress and difficulties in prayer, ¶ the method and material of our mental prayer, ¶ our spiritual aspirations and ideals, ¶ the leadings of the Holy Spirit, ¶ our physical and mental health, ¶ our work, ¶ our social life, ¶ our school and home activities—in brief, he should know everything that brings us to God, that

194

takes us from Him, that can be made to do one or the other.

Ejaculatory Prayers

Short aspirations can be used to sum up the ideas and inspirations of the day's mental prayer and to maintain an atmosphere of recollection throughout a busy day.

Holy Trinity, one God, have mercy on us.
[500 days, R. 26]

From all sin deliver me, O Lord.   [500 days, R. 27]

Thy will be done!   [500 days, R. 32]

Lord, I am my own enemy, when I seek my peace apart from You.   [300 days, R. 35]

Lord, increase our faith.   [500 days, R. 38]

My God, I love You.   [300 days, R. 39]

My Jesus, mercy.   [300 days, R. 70]

Sweetest Jesus, be not my Judge, but my Savior.
[300 days, R. 71]

Blessed be the most holy name of Jesus without end!
[300 days, R. 119]

Praise and adoration ever more be given to the most Holy Sacrament.   [300 days, R. 135]

My Jesus, I believe that You are present in the Blessed Sacrament. I love You above all things and wish to receive You into my soul. Since I cannot receive You sacramentally, come at least spiritually into my heart.

[To the faithful who make an act of spiritual Communion, using any formula they choose, is granted an indulgence of 3 years, R. 164]

195

Hail, O cross, our only hope.   [500 days, R. 187]

Heart of Jesus, I put my trust in You!
[300 days, R. 226]

Sacred Heart of Jesus, protect our families.
[300 days, R. 236]

Jesus, Mary, Joseph!   [7 years, R. 274]

O Mary, Virgin Mother of God, pray to Jesus for me.
[300 days, R. 305]

O Saint Joseph, foster father of our Lord Jesus Christ
and true spouse of Mary the Virgin, pray for us.
[300 days, R. 459]

Notes on Gaining Indulgences

To gain the many indulgences possible each day,
make a general intention each morning, such as: "I wish
to gain all the indulgences attached to the prayers I shall
say and the good works I shall perform today."

Though a person can gain practically every indulgence for his own benefit (but never for the benefit of
any other living person), they may be equally offered
for the relief of the poor souls in purgatory. Unless a
general intention is made in favor of these poor souls,
indulgences will be applied to oneself.

General conditions for gaining indulgences: A person
must be validly baptized; not excommunicated; in the
state of grace (if gaining the indulgence for himself) at
least when the last condition is fulfilled; must have in-
tended with at least a general intention to gain the indulgence. No special conditions are normally attached to
gaining partial indulgences.

Usual conditions for plenary indulgences:
1 Confession any time within eight full days before
   or after the day of gaining the indulgence.
2 Holy Communion any time within one day before
   or eight full days after gaining the indulgence.

196

3 Visit to a church either on the day on which the
work is performed or the afternoon of the pre-
ceding day.
4 Prayers for the intentions of the holy father, which
condition is fulfilled by saying one Our Father,
Hail Mary, and Glory be.

And when day broke, he summoned
his disciples; and from these he chose
twelve (whom he also named apostles).
Luke 6:13

The Apostolate

✝

I have chosen you.
Your vocation is not only to personal sanctification.
Your vocation also includes a mission,
a mission to bring others under My standard,
to strengthen My body, the Church,
to spread the Christ-life,
to be an apostle.
This is part of the challenge.

I ask you to join My apostles,
Peter and Paul and the others who helped Me
establish My Church;
Patrick and Boniface who extended My kingdom
to pagan lands;
the monks of the Middle Ages who preserved
Christianity for you;
the Crusaders who fought the heathens for
possession of My Holy Land;
the North American martyrs whose blood
nourished the growth of My Church on your soil;

197

the modern missionaries who are still laboring
   to extend My kingdom;
your fellow Christians throughout the world
   who by living an apparently ordinary life
   are yet My missionaries, My apostles.

I could have touched the hearts of men
   by My grace alone.
I could have chosen only My ordained priests
   to be apostles.
But I have chosen you to share My work.
I need you, I depend on you.
The salvation of a soul may depend on you.
The higher perfection of many souls
   will depend on you.

For you,
you are My apostle,
just as you are.
You need not be a Xavier,
bringing Me to distant pagan lands,
but I ask you to bring Me daily
to your family and friends.
You need not be a Brebeuf,
burning at an Indian stake,
but through your sufferings
you can spread belief in Me.
You need not die for Me
as Catholics in Spain not many years ago,
in Germany still more recently,
in China and Russia today.
But if I ask, you must live for Me,
live an ordinary life, still as My apostle.

For there is much in an ordinary life that
   can be apostolic:

your example to others,
your attitude toward sin,
your conversation,
your self-control,
your leadership in studies and work,
your cooperation in Catholic Action.
In your daily life watch and study Me.
I will show you how to labor.
I will be at your side in everything that you do,
your words will be My words,
your work will be My work.

I carried on My apostolate wherever I was—
among the fishermen of Galilee I was a fisherman,
in the city of Jerusalem I taught the word of God,
in Samaria I went as a missionary to the ignorant.
Like Me, you, too, must be an apostle
wherever you find yourself:
in your home, in your school,
in your social life, in your recreation,
in your parish.

The life of a Christian is a life of
knowing Me, his Creator and Redeemer,
loving Me, his leader and friend,
serving Me, his master and his God.
The Christian serves Me by bringing to others
this knowledge of Me,
this love of Me,
this desire of Me.

I did not wait for men to come to Me.
I traveled the roads of Judea
calling men to repent of their sins,
calling them to a knowledge of God, their Father,
to a life of perfection, a life following Me.

Now this mission is your mission.
You, My apostle, must go to others.
You must not wait for them to come to you.
I have given you everything you have.
Now I ask you in return to give it to others:
your knowledge of My love,
your love of My Person,
your desire to do everything for Me.

INSTRUCTION ON THE APOSTOLATE

Apostolic-mindedness

The word *apostle* means one who is sent. In Scripture and in all subsequent Christian literature the word is used to describe one sent by God to other men in order to help bring them a share in divine truth and a share in divine life. Because the Catholic is a member of the Church and united to our Lord through sanctifying grace, he is a member of the mystical body of Christ, which is the Church. As a member of the living mystical body of Christ, he is a kind of prolongation of Christ. Christ's life on earth was essentially apostolic, aimed at teaching divine truth and bringing a share in divine life, sanctifying grace. The life of a member of Christ must also be apostolic, else he can in no sense be said to be prolonging the life of Christ.

Just as Christ's physical body had members and functions, so has His mystical body:

members—all those who are baptized, who profess the true faith, and who are not separated from the unity of the Body;

function—prolong the life of Christ by teaching divine truth, by helping to bring divine life.

The Catholic must, then, be conscious of this vital connection he has to all other souls in the Church. He must realize that he is not alone in his sharing of Christ's life, sanctifying grace, but that he is an individual element united with all the other elements into one functioning organism, the mystical body of Christ.

200

Because of this vital connection between all the souls in the Church, a Catholic's holiness may be personal but it can never be private. The condition of his soul will always affect the rest of the Church. For him to commit deliberate sin is a sad way for him to treat our Lord. Such an act does harm to his personal holiness, but it also hurts the grace-life of the whole Church. Another member of the mystical body may be harmfully affected if he fails to keep his love for Christ sincere and dynamic. On the other hand, when a Catholic is faithful to his personal duties toward our Lord, he helps strengthen and enrich the entire organism of the Church.

The Catholic, therefore, must be apostolic-minded. He must be conscious of the needs and temptations of the other souls in the Church, and he must be desirous of helping them by apostolic work and prayer.

The Apostolate of the Interior Life of Grace

The interior life of grace and the apostolic life of helping to bring grace to others are two sides of one and the same love of God:

the interior life—a love of God in Himself,

the apostolate—a love of God in others.

The interior life and the apostolate complement one another. By the interior life—prayer and the sacraments and the practice of Christian virtue—the Catholic is united to our Lord. He thus nourishes the Christ-life within him. Because of this every action is performed together with and in Christ. Our Lord and he spend their days together and the love that is shared by them grows stronger and more dynamic. Because he is Christ-like he is concerned for the salvation of all the other souls in the world. He burns with an apostolic fire to bring all men under the banner of Christ the King.

By the apostolate the Catholic brings Christ to others. His love of Christ urges him to bring, as much as he can, the thrilling life of grace to others, but he soon realizes that his efficiency and success in the apostolate depend, in turn, upon the closeness and vitality of his own union with Christ. Faced at times with almost overwhelming odds and the grim specter of failure, the apostle develops great trust in God, deep humility, and an ever growing love for souls and sympathy with them. He will learn self-control and mortification in the most severe of schools and will thus be enabled to uproot in himself the weeds of selfishness, egoism, pride, and self-indulgence which are the chief obstacles to a truly vigorous interior life.

Thus, there seems to be not two objectives—personal holiness and apostolate—but one objective with a twofold aspect.

Forms of the Apostolate

In general we can list two main types of apostolate:

1 *Direct*: Explicitly to teach others the truths of the Church, to give another a share in divine life through the sacraments.
2 *Indirect*: To prepare the way for the actual reception of the truths of the Church and the reception of divine life by: witness and example of a Christian life, engaging in the spiritual works of mercy, engaging in the corporal works of mercy.

Recent popes have insisted that the laity share the apostolate. Their cooperation is more often indirect, occasionally direct, as in emergency baptism.

There are two ways to engage in apostolic work: on an individual basis and as a member of an apostolic group project:

Individual or personal apostolate: The Catholic on his own seeks for opportunities to be an apostle. He does not have to seek far—his own family, school, business associates, friends, and even strangers. His attitudes, example, opportune remarks are the instruments he uses. If he is united with our Lord, he will be eminently successful and our Lord will act through him.

Group apostolate: The Catholic joins an apostolic organization, such as the Sodality. He is banded together with his fellow members for a very definite reason: together they can accomplish what would be impossible for each one alone. As has been said, "The organization of the good is the multiplication of the good."

One form of this group apostolate which is deserving of special mention is the so-called "institutional apostolate" or "social apostolate." As a group Catholics can affect those institutions which so strongly influence the lives of men. An institution, as we are using the term, is any one of those numberless ways of thinking and behaving on the part of a large segment of men which are more or less permanent and fulfill some human need. Some institutions would be the family, race relations, politics, labor unions, schools, and so on. Each organization or group will decide to what particular sphere of influence it will devote itself, depending on the particular need of the environment. Then it will fall to the zeal of the individual members to carry on the work to completion. Attendance at meetings, serious planning, and devoted application of one's talents and efforts will be of the utmost importance if the goal is to be achieved. It may be that a particular apostolate, though decided upon by the group, will not appeal to some members. In such a case they must subordinate their own interests to the interest of the group, and consider the sacrifice one of the necessary ones for a successful apostolic effort.

Conclusion

Apostolic Christians have *More* emblazoned on their battle flag. They will always be conscious of the needs of their fellow men. They will always be searching for new and more effective ways of strengthening the mystical body of Christ and of bringing Christ to souls. When this apostolic consciousness becomes the driving force of the Christian's life, then he can truly say with the great apostle Saint Paul:

> It is now no longer
> I that live
> but Christ lives
> in me.

Prayer for Peace

Lord, make me an instrument of Your peace. Where there is hatred, let me sow love; where there is injury, pardon; where there is doubt, faith; where there is despair, hope; where there is darkness, light; and where there is sadness, joy.

O divine Master, grant that I may not so much seek to be consoled as to console; to be understood as to understand; to be loved as to love; for it is in giving that we receive; it is in pardoning that we are pardoned; and it is in dying that we are born to eternal life.   Saint Francis of Assisi

The Spirit of an Apostle

Dear Jesus, give me the spirit of an apostle. Let me be filled with a desire to influence others for Your sake. May my goal in life be not just to keep the treasure of the faith, but to bring it to others. Help me to remember that no one lives his life alone, but always helps others either to heaven or hell. Let me so live, Lord, that the world may be a better place for my having lived in it.

Dear Lord, give me a world view of things. Keep me from getting confined to myself and my own little problems. Enlarge my horizon with Your greatness and Your vision. Let me see it as You saw it, as You died, hanging on the cross for all men. Amen.

Prayer for Apostles

Give us courage and enthusiasm, give us charity and unity, give us a spirit of initiative and originality of thought. ¶ Give us a pure intention in everything and a deep love for the cross; give us a thirst for souls. ¶ Deliver us from selfishness and jealousy, deliver us from cowardice and the fear of making sacrifices; deliver us from blindness toward the need of our neighbors; deliver us from deafness toward the inspirations of the Holy Spirit.   Author unknown

Prayer to Saint Paul

Saint Paul, help us in the work on the street corner to see in every aimless question a human soul groping in the dark for truth; in every conceited declaration, a human soul desperately grasping for the dignity of which it has been robbed; in every aggressive challenge, a human soul steeped in the conflict between this world and the next; in every angry denial, a human soul shrinking from the sacrifice of the cross; in every false statement, a human soul lost on the road through ignorance; in every feigned difficulty, a human soul misled by false prophets; in every scornful laugh, a human soul deprived of the only real joy; and in every listener, the image and likeness of God. Amen.   McAniff

Favorite Prayer of Saint Francis Xavier, Apostle of the Indies

O God, the everlasting Creator of all things, remember that the souls of unbelievers have been created by You and formed in Your own image and likeness. ¶ Remember that Your Son Jesus endured a most painful death for their salvation. ¶ Permit not, I beseech You, Lord, that Your Son should be any longer despised by unbelievers. ¶ But be appeased by the prayers of saintly men and of the Church, the spouse of Your most holy Son, and be mindful of Your mercy. ¶ Forget their idolatry and unbelief and bring it about that they too may some day acknowledge Him whom You have sent, Jesus Christ, Your Son, our Lord, who is our salvation, our life and resurrection, by whom we have been saved and delivered, to whom be glory for endless ages. Amen.

[500 days, R. 612]

Prayer to the Jesuit Martyr-Saints of North America

Protect our land, O heavenly patrons, which you have bedewed with the rich treasure of your blood. Watch over our Catholic faith which you helped to establish in this new land. Bring all our fellow citizens to a knowledge and love of the truth. Make us zealous in spreading abroad a knowledge of Catholic teachings, so that we may continue and perfect the work which you have begun with so much labor and suffering. Pray for our homes, our schools, our missions, for vocations, for the conversion of sinners, the return of those who wandered from the fold, and the perseverance of all the faithful. Amen.

Author unknown

For the Propagation of the Faith

God, who desires that all men should be saved and that all should come to know the truth, we pray You send forth laborers to Your harvest and give them strength to proclaim Your word with all confidence, so that Your teaching may be received with honor throughout the world and all nations may acknowledge You, the true and only God, and Him whom You have sent, Jesus Christ, Your Son, our Lord; who is God. Amen.   [R. 615]

Invocation for Unity

That You would bring back into the unity of the Church all that stray, and lead all unbelievers to the light of the Gospel, we beseech You to hear us, O Lord.   [300 days, R. 621]

Prayer to Saint Thérèse

Dear Saint Thérèse, chosen by the Church as the heavenly patroness of the missions, we ask you to take under your special protection those valiant souls who have left family, home, friends—all that the human heart holds dear—in order to spread the kingdom of Christ.

When you lived on earth your soul reached out to those soldiers of the cross. Day after day you prayed for them, you suffered for them, you made them and their work the core of your whole life. Today you are in heaven. Today you see Jesus face to face. Since you understand the needs of our modern missionaries, remember them to their Leader and their Lord. Beg Jesus to give them courage to fight even when they can see no reward, to rely on Him for their comfort and peace. Beg Him to bless their work that they might spread everywhere His kingdom, for that is their life and their joy and their goal. Saint Thérèse, we trust in you. Amen.

Prayer of Church Unity Octave

Antiphon: That they all may be one, as You, Father, in Me and I in You; that they also may be one in Us; that the world may believe that You have sent Me.

I say to you that you are Peter;
And upon this rock I will build My Church.

O Lord Jesus Christ, who said to Your apostles: Peace I leave with you, My peace I give to you, regard not our sins, but the faith of Your Church, and grant her that peace and unity which are agreeable to Your will, who lives and reigns God for ever and ever. Amen.   [300 days during octave, R. 622]

Prayer for Priests

Keep them, I pray Thee, dearest Lord,
Keep them for they are Thine,
Thy priests whose lives burn out before
Thy consecrated shrine.
Keep them—Thou knowest, dearest Lord—
The world, the flesh are strong,
And Satan spreads a thousand snares
To lead them into wrong.
Keep them for they are in the world
Though from the world apart;
When earthly pleasures tempt, allure,
Shelter them in Thy heart.
Keep them, and comfort them in hours
Of loneliness and pain
When all their life of sacrifice
For souls seems but in vain.
Keep them, and O remember, Lord,
They have no one but Thee—
Yet they have only human hearts
With human frailty.
Keep them as spotless as the host
That daily they caress—
Their every thought and word and deed
Deign, dearest Lord, to bless.

Author unknown

Invocations

O Mary, Queen of the clergy, pray for us; obtain
for us many and holy priests. Amen.

[300 days, R. 604]

O God, who has appointed Your only-begotten Son
to be the eternal high priest for the glory of Your
majesty and the salvation of mankind; grant that
they whom He has chosen to be His ministers and

the stewards of His mysteries may be found faithful in the fulfillment of the ministry which they have received.   [3 years, R. 660]

In Gratitude—A Prayer for Nuns

Bless, O Lord, all the nuns throughout the world. People of every kind—the ignorant, the penniless, the sick and dying, the homeless, the aged, the young— all have experienced the generous help, the smiling kindness of a nun. As Veronica of Jerusalem consoled You on the Way of the Cross, so these selfless women today console You in the needy souls of every walk in life. In gratitude for what they have done for the world and for me in particular, I ask You to bless them always with Your peace and joy and grace. Amen.

For the Conversion of Non-Catholics

O immaculate Virgin, who by a singular privilege of grace was preserved from the stain of original sin, cast a glance of pity upon our separated brethren. Recall them to the center of unity, so that they, too, may be your sons. In many cases, although separated, they still keep in their hearts a sentiment of love for you. In your generosity, reward them and obtain for them their conversion.

From the very beginning of your existence, you were victorious over the powers of hell. O Mary, will you not use your power with God to triumph over the infernal enemy? Will you not add to the glory of your Son by bringing back to the great Shepherd the sheep that have gone astray?

May it be to your glory, O holy Virgin, to destroy all error and to restore unity and peace to all Christian peoples. Amen.   [R. 627]

Oblation for the Missions

O God of love! In all humility and confidence I offer
You the Immaculate Heart of Mary together with
the loving Heart of Jesus our Lord, who gave Himself upon the cross of Calvary and still offers Himself
upon the altar to sanctify and save the souls of men.
In loving union with this sacrifice of infinite value,
I offer You my whole being, O my God, and all my
prayers and sufferings, all my sorrows and labors,
my life and death, in order to fulfill Your divine will
in my own soul, to sanctify all missionaries and their
native clergy, to obtain the grace of perseverance
for their converts as well as the conversion of all
sinners and unbelievers in their missions. Amen.

[500 days, R. 616]

---

*. . . walk . . . worthy of the calling with
which you were called.*
Ephesians 4:1

✝ Vocation

Many times you have knelt before Me,
many times you have asked,
"Lord, what do You want me to do?"
There is only one answer I can give:
study My own life upon earth,
see that My great desire was to do the will of
My Father,
understand that My food and My drink was
to do His will.
You must be like Me,

You must prolong My life
by your grace-life,
by your Christ-life.
You must imitate Me,
and extend My life into the twentieth century,
especially My obedience to My Father,
especially My desire to do His holy will.
It is of extreme importance that you discover
    God's will
in regard to your future state of life.
For if you discover
and if you follow your true vocation,
you will win deeper happiness in this life,
you will be more certain of fuller happiness
    in the next,
you will most certainly be answering My challenge.
To know your vocation you must investigate,
you must consult,
you must pray.
If you do these things,
My Father will reveal to you His plans.
He will not unveil them all at once.
He will probably give you light only for
    the next step.
He will not send an angel to enlighten you.
He will probably use ordinary, everyday means.
But rest assured: He will reveal His plans.
The rest is up to you:
you must follow the light He gives,
you must embrace the life He desires for you.
Then you too can say:
"My meat is to do the will of Him who sent me
and to accomplish the task He gave me."
I put Adam in the garden of Eden,
but I did not leave him alone.
It is not good for man to be alone.

So I created a mate for him.
Thus, it was I who created the two sexes.
I made them both in My own likeness,
and I knew they were good.

Increase and multiply, I told them.
It was My will that they should bring children
    into the world
and that their children should have children.
A man shall leave father and mother
and shall cleave to his wife,
and they shall be two in one flesh.
Thus, marriage is good because I instituted it—
    it was My will.

When I walked the earth
I showed the divine approval of marriage.
I went to the marriage of a couple in Cana.
If my command "increase and multiply" is
    to be carried out,
there must be men and women courageous enough
    to undertake the hardships of the married life,
to work with Me in the creation of new souls.

To many souls, for reasons which are Mine alone,
for My ways are not your ways,
I have given no vocation to marriage,
no desire to unite themselves with another.
I have given no call to the priesthood or to religion,
no desire to dedicate themselves to Me
in holy orders, or
through the three vows of religion.

All through the ages
I have asked men and women to serve Me
by remaining alone in the world.

It is not because they remain alone
that they serve Me better,
but remaining alone
they find it easier to center their hearts on Me alone.
Setting aside the intimate companionship
    of marriage,
they choose Me for their companion through life.
They dedicate their virginity and all
    their virtues to Me,
and Me alone they shall have for their reward
for all eternity.

I am pleased when a person wants to serve Me
as a married man or woman.
I am pleased when a person wants to serve Me
in the single state.
But the most exalted state
is that wherein a person consecrates himself
wholly and irrevocably to Me
by his priestly or religious vows.
I invite My friends to this life.
You do not choose Me,
I choose you.
I choose you because I love you.
I call you to this life
because it is the imitation of My life upon earth.
My great gift is the call to this life of
    close companionship.
Blessed is the man who hears this call!

Instruction on Vocation

A vocation is a call from God to a particular state
or manner of life in which a person is to save his soul and
fill the needs of the Church of Christ. The vocation-call
is a supernatural grace: it is a divine light to understand
the needs of the Church and how one's own abilities

measure up to those needs, and it is a gentle urge on the heart to fill those needs of the Church to the full measure of his ability. With this gentle grace from God there may come a feeling of generosity, the sense that religion or the married state is the best thing for me, for others, and for the Church. But this feeling is not necessary; as long as we know what the Church needs, as long as we are reasonably sure that our abilities lie in this or that direction, then, once we have willed to enter one rather than another state of life—that state is our vocation.

How are we to judge our abilities? There are three general fields of classification: the physical, the intellectual, and the moral. Physically, the person choosing a state of life must be capable of performing the ordinary duties of that state. For instance, the man who chooses to marry must be capable of performing the marital act; moreover, he must be capable of supporting his wife and children. The man who chooses the priesthood must have a sound enough body to take the difficulties of a long period of training. The woman who wishes to dedicate her life to God in a sisterhood must have sufficiently good health to carry out the ordinary duties of the institute she wants to join.

Intellectually, few persons are incapable of undertaking the married or the single life. The person entering the priestly life must be able to study for some years after high school. Teaching sisters also, for instance, must do further academic work.

Morally, the requirements for each of the states is the same: the person must be willing and able to practice the characteristic virtues of the state he enters. For the married state patience, prudence, purity, and unselfish love are, perhaps, characteristic; for the single state faith, kindness, purity, and piety; for religious love of God, zeal, poverty, chastity, and obedience.

In general, then, a vocation is a solid desire in the will and a right intention in the mind, joined to those qualities of body and soul which make the aspirant a fit

214

candidate for one or the other of the states in life. Every Christian, certainly, has a vocation. Through his state in life, which God has chosen for him, he must save his own soul, and fill the needs of God and His Church.

Marriage

Marriage is the ordinary vocation of most men and women. It is a permanent union of one man and one woman, having a twofold purpose: to work with God in creating new souls, to aid one another in working out their eternal salvation.

Marriage is a sacrament. Therefore it is instituted by Christ as a means of grace for the partners of the marriage. It is a state in life which is holy and highly pleasing to God.

Marriage is based on mutual love and reverence. This love is physical, psychological, and supernatural—the surrender of one's body, mind, and soul. All three loves are needed for a complete and holy marriage.

Physical love is a natural attraction of the sexes, implanted by God and, therefore, good. It is fundamental, but not the most important element in marriage. Physical love, the fulfillment of the natural desire to love and be loved, is the expression, in acts, of the spiritual and intellectual union of the partners. The Catholic attitude toward sex is based on reverence toward the body as a temple of the Holy Spirit. The Catholic regards sex as a creature of God, to be used in the way He desires, for His purposes and not merely pleasure. Through physical love a man and his wife cooperate with God in the creation of another person; from this flows the real beauty of marital love.

Psychological love is a blending of ambitions, ideals, and interests into a common life. Their primary ambition is their desire for children, their wish to make a real home. But permeating all of their desires is their ambition to work for everything together. Together they will find their way to heaven; together they will sanctify their life and their love; together they will make of their children perfect Christians—these are their ideals. Psychological love demands not only common ambitions and ideals but even a sharing of ordinary interests. He must find time for her home and social activities, she must find interest in his work. Together they must share the most fundamental of all their interests, their love of religion and the Church. Indeed, they must share everything, surrendering to each other their whole minds, their whole hearts.

Supernatural love consists in the union of husband and wife with Christ through each other. In drawing closer to one another they must draw closer to Christ. The soul of each should be a mirror in which the other may contemplate the image and likeness of God. Thus their married life is a co-consecration, a growing holy together as the years pass.

Marriage, as a sublime vocation, is the sharing in that love which Christ has for His Church. Marriage is a sharing in the divine powers of creation by the acts proper to the married state; of providence by providing for the children of the marriage; of priesthood as sanctifiers of the home; of teacher by instructing one another by their love and charity; of kingship by wielding the authority of God as parents.

Marriage, as God intends it, is a beautiful, sanctifying state. It is the surrendering of one's body, mind, and heart to a lover in order that, through this surrender, the couple may praise, reverence, and serve God and through the fulfillment of His will gain life everlasting.

The Single State

Another possible state in life is the single state, a state pleasing to God if by means of it a person devotes his heart and mind more fully to God. The single person does not undertake the added responsibilities of the religious or married state. But this does not mean that his lot is necessarily easier; in the priestly state a man finds a great deal of excellent guidance to help him, and the same may be said of the intimate companionship of man and wife in the married state. This guidance and companionship are not as characteristically abundant in the single state. The person who chooses the single state chooses to undertake all the difficulties of a Christian life in a sin-filled world—alone. Nonetheless, with the graces of this state from an all-loving God, it is possible to live a very perfect life in the single state, and to attain a close intimacy with the Heart of Jesus.

The Church needs lay apostles just as she needs apostolic priests. There are some people in need who cannot be reached by a priest, and there are some necessary jobs which cannot be done by priests or men consecrated exclusively to the service of God. The Church must have lay apostles. It is clear that the single person, who is not tied down by the responsibilities of supporting a wife and children, is freer than the married person to fill this urgent need for lay apostles.

What are the signs of a vocation to the single state? Certainly fear of accepting the responsibilities and difficulties of either of the other two states is not a sign of a vocation to the single state. However, a disinclination to marry or to enter the priesthood or religious life, or a distinct lack of the qualifications for either of these states, seems to be one of the signs. Join this to a desire to remain alone in the world serving God and His Church, and this seems to be a vocation to the single state.

It should be noticed that a person living in the single state may want to consecrate by private vow his virginity or some other Christian virtue. Saint Paul praised this kind of act, and many of the saints of the Church have lived such consecrated lives.

Priestly and Religious Vocation

The long tradition of the Church teaches us that dedicating one's life completely to the service of God is the most perfect way of life. There are two main ways of serving God in this life of dedication: either as a member of a religious order or congregation or secular institute, or as a member of the diocesan priesthood. The vows of religion are poverty, by which an individual gives up the right to independent use of material goods; chastity, by which a person promises not to marry; obedience, by which a person binds himself to obey the commands of his superiors. The diocesan priest takes a vow of chastity and makes a solemn promise of obedience to the bishop of his diocese.

Every call, therefore, to this more perfect way of life is not a call to the same type of life. For instance, a Jesuit lay brother is a religious but not a priest; a Jesuit priest is a religious and a priest; a diocesan priest is a priest but not a religious. All, however, serve the same Master. All embrace an exalted vocation. All have accepted Christ's invitation, "Come, follow Me."

Not everybody is called to this life, nor is everybody fitted for it. Those aspiring to the priesthood must meet certain requirements. They must have normal good health and ability to learn; they must be of good moral character and truly desire to be a priest of Christ. A vocation is not a matter of feeling—it is a calling of grace. God freely gives to certain men the invitation to keep alive the precious heritage of the Sacrifice and the sacraments. God also gives the grace to accept the invitation He has offered.

For those who might desire to serve God as a Brother or a Sister, the requirements, in general, are similar to those for the priesthood, but frequently less stringent. Each order, congregation, or institute will have different requirements depending on its particular purpose. It should be noted that there are certain things which might render the religious life too difficult for some people. For example: habits of sin which are not sufficiently overcome, extreme nervousness, moods of depression, and so forth. Hence, it is extremely important that anyone who feels that he or she has a call to serve God in this special way should discuss the matter with a priest, in the confessional or at a private interview.

The life is not easy, but God has told us that His grace is sufficient for us. He has told us that we too must

218

take up our crosses if we wish to merit heaven, that He will reward us for this heroic act of love.

"Amen I say to you . . .
everyone who has left house,
or brothers, or sisters, or father, or mother, or wife,
or children, or lands,
for my name's sake,
shall receive
a hundredfold,
and shall possess life everlasting"
(Matthew 19:28-29).

Prayer for Choosing a State of Life

O my God, who are the God of wisdom and of counsel, who reads in my heart the sincere will to please You alone, and to govern myself with regard to my choice of a state of life entirely in conformity with Your most holy desire; grant me, by the intercession of the most Blessed Virgin, my mother, and of my holy patrons, the grace to know what state I ought to choose, and when known, to embrace it, so that in it I may be able to pursue and increase Your glory, work out my salvation, and merit that heavenly reward which You have promised to those who do Your holy will. Amen.   [300 days, R. 711]

Prayer for Light

Shine the light of Your grace, O Lord, to guide my weary feet along Your path. Does it matter where it leads or what comes upon me as I make my way? No, Lord. I only ask this: may it always be Your road, may it always lead to You. Send whatever You will, whatever suffering or doubt. Give me only this, a true and sturdy heart that yearns for You alone.

You have led me thus far. I know that if I ask You will continue to guide me, to bring me further until I reach the end. Never leave me, Lord, because I am Yours and I want You to be mine. For You alone are my God, my most holy God, my most pure God, my most merciful God. Amen.

Prayer for the Right Partner in Life

Dear Jesus, I know now that You are calling me to serve You in the married state. I know, too, that it is a life that calls for self-sacrifice, courage, and the guidance of the Holy Spirit. It will not be easy to live as a true Catholic parent, to put the interests of You and Your Church before those of my sometimes selfish heart. But, Lord, I know You will give me all the graces to live as a holy and happily married Catholic. Of all these graces, Lord, the greatest for which I can ask is the right partner who will share with me all I have, all I am, and all I will be. Guide me in my choice, Jesus. Help me fall in love with the one person You know will be best for me. Give me the person who will strengthen me through life's tears and inspire me to see all the goodness and happiness of two people living their life together with You, their dear God, in their midst. Amen.

Consecration of Courtship

Remember, O most blessed Mother, that never was it known that anyone who fled to your protection, implored your help, or sought your intercession was left unaided. Inspired with this confidence, unworthy as I am of your protection, in the presence of God the Father, the author of life, of God the Son, who gave marriage the dignity of a sacrament, of God the Holy Spirit, who sanctifies marital love, I, (NAME), entrust my courtship to your motherly protection. Guide me in the choice of a partner. Keep my courtship pure and chaste. Bless our union with a holy love. Watch over us from heaven. Send us grace to live in the favor of God and to share in the eternal love in which we shall be united forever in heaven. Amen.   O'Flaherty

Prayer for Religious Vocations for Girls

Dearest Mother, my mother, I come to you today with a mind and a heart full of need. Tell me, Mary, what does God want of me? As you once called yourself His "handmaid," and He made His will known to you, so, too, do I call myself today His handmaid. Will you beg Him then, to make His will clear for me as well? Is He really asking me to become His bride, to assist in the spreading of His kingdom? If so, then I want to follow Him. Please, dear Mother, ask Him to clear my mind of doubt and hesitation so that I might be able to walk along the path He points out for me.

I know well that if mine is the grace of a special vocation it will cost. But I am willing and eager to do everything I ought to pay the price. He may be asking me to give up many things that a woman holds dear, but I know that in return I will receive a hundredfold. I will have Him; I will have the house of God for my own. I will have children of the spirit: those children whom I will teach, counsel, encourage, reprimand, and soothe; all those for whom I will pray and suffer and for whom I will spend my life. I plead now for only this, Mother: to be given the insight to know His will, the will to accept it, and then the strength to live always as one who has given herself—body and soul, heart and mind—to her Lord, her God, to her Jesus and yours. Amen.

Vocational Prayer for the Brothers

Lord Jesus, I know You are not calling me to the priesthood. Still, I feel that You want me to give myself to You in a special way, the way of the religious brotherhood. Enlighten my mind to see clearly what You are asking. Strengthen my will that Your desires become mine. Help me love and appreciate the meaning of this special vocation of service to Your Church and her priests. Widen my heart so that I might be able to labor for You selflessly and constantly. Though the work You may ask me to do is hidden, I know that in it I will find You. Though the world may never hear of me, my name will be written forever in Your Heart. Though I be asked to turn away from the pleasures and happiness of this world, I know that I will find that joy which will never fade away or turn to sorrow, the joy of God Himself. Lord, if this is the life which You are holding out to me, I willingly reach out and grasp it and make it my own. Amen.

Prayer of a Married Couple

Lord Jesus, at the marriage feast of Cana You performed Your first public miracle. By that wonderful token of interest, regard, and deep affection, You showed all the world for all time how You, our God, viewed marriage. Look down today, Jesus, on this our marriage. Bless us both. Help us carry out the grave but happy responsibility of this our vocation. Teach us to see life with Your eyes, to see the worth of one immortal soul, to live in mutual love. In our difficulties never let us doubt one another or ourselves. Help us trust in Your grace. Help us cherish those ideals which You hold out to us in the teachings of Your Church. Give us, if it is Your will, a share in Your creation by making us parents. Please show us how to guide our children, how to love them. Make our home, Jesus, Your home, a home of joy and peace. What we are really asking is this: make our marriage complete through Your presence in us and with us. Amen.

Prayer of an Unmarried Person

I am not called to be one of Your religious, Jesus, yet I know I can still give my life to You. I am not drawn to the married life, still I realize that I have a place in the larger family of mankind. Help me fulfill both these obligations. To You I dedicate my chastity. Guard it that I might live with a pure heart and a clean body in the midst of the world. Teach me to do all my work out of love for You. Help me turn to You more and more, to make the interests of Your Church my interests. Teach me, too, to live for others. Please never allow me to become selfish. Let every eye that falls on me see Your virtues, Jesus—Your charity, Your humility, Your kindness, Your strength, Your peace and joy of heart. Make me, Jesus, another Jesus that I might lead all men to You. Amen.

In the Ranks of Christ

In this age of Mary, more than ever before, my Creator and God, it is clear to me that You are calling great numbers of young men, like myself, to become priests and brothers—special soldiers in the army of Christ. I see the forces of evil drawn up, ready to strike in a final, all-out attempt to enslave forever the souls which Jesus bought by His blood and death on the cross. I do not wish to sit back in this crucial hour of history, but I desire to throw myself wholeheartedly into the battle. By the light of the Holy Spirit show me where You want me to fight. Grant that it be in the ranks of Your Son; and if so, give me the courage and direction to offer myself to the proper seminary, there to begin my training as a priest or brother to fight and dwell forever at the side of Your divine Son. Amen.

The Priest

To live in the midst of the world, without wishing its pleasures; to be a member of each family, yet belonging to none; to share all sufferings, to penetrate all secrets, to heal all wounds; to go from men to God and offer Him their prayers; to return from God to men and bring them His pardon and hope; to have a heart of fire for charity and a heart of bronze for chastity; always to teach and to forgive, to console and to bless. Merciful God, what an exalted life! And it is yours, O Priest of Jesus Christ!

Lacordaire

The Future

✝

Many centuries ago in Judea,
a young man came to Me and asked,
Good Master, what shall I do to gain eternal life?
I answered him:
One thing is lacking to you;
go, sell whatever you have,
and give to the poor, and
you will have treasures in heaven;
and come, follow Me.

I watched with sad eyes and heavy heart that day
as the young man turned away puzzled
and walked slowly down the road.
He was afraid to cast in his lot with Me,
for he had great possessions.
Many have I seen through the centuries retrace
   the same unhappy path.

Others have spared Me that pain—as you have.
Your story—
the story of those enlisted in My company
under the special banner of My Mother—
your story has a ringing, triumphant note.
For you have heard My invitation
and have eagerly answered it.
You have said, or intend soon to say:

"Lord, I am with You.
Perhaps You have not given me treasures of money,
but You have bestowed upon me treasures of a
    different, far greater sort.
You have given me Your love and Your grace,
the power to live Your life,
to reflect Your personality,
to be to some extent another Christ to all I meet.
And those treasures I am going to give to the poor,
to the poorest of all,
those who have You not.
You did not give them to me to hoard miserlike for
    myself alone.
This wealth I am going to share with all men
along whatever path of life You want me to walk."

Following Christ

We have given the Heart of Christ great joy by our generous enlistment in His ranks. Under His leadership, we are eager to take our special places in the line of march. But before we begin the journey, should we not step aside for a moment to consider the terrain over which He intends to go? Would it not be prudent to see what lies ahead, to understand what our eager enlistment may imply in terms of service? We must have our feet planted on firm ground and not walk with our heads in the clouds. We cannot afford to march into a dream world armed with mere empty enthusiasm.

Christ is supremely honest. His own life, as those of His best imitators, the saints, is proof enough that pain and hardship are part of His way. He holds out no false, unrealistic hopes to those who want to follow His standard. The plight of His faithful followers even in our twentieth century shows that suspicion, persecution, imprisonment, and even death are not beyond expectation for the Catholic.

Nor would He have us deceived concerning the ordinary events of life. Certainly, thus far in life we have suffered somewhat—aches and pains, sicknesses, small disappointments, perhaps even separation by death from our most beloved. Look at the older people around us. They have not been spared the ordinary sorrows of life. Following Christ, the Man of Sorrows, does not insure that such events will be no more.

Are these hard facts, the realities of life which will befall us, to make us lose heart?

Christ Our Courage

In the face of every hard fact, there is another fact that the Catholic should never forget: by his dedication to his Lord and His Mother, he has assured himself of never really facing a future crisis alone. Always he will have the only vital necessity in life: always he will have Christ.

For if Christ did not absolutely promise His followers things which they perhaps would enjoy—wealth, a long life, no sorrow, always a return of love from those whom they love, the faithfulness of friends, good health, popularity, even visible success in the great work of furthering His kingdom—He did promise them Himself. He did say:

> Peace I leave with you,
> My peace I give to you;
> not as the world gives do I give to you.
> Do not let your heart be troubled
> or be afraid.

With the unshakable spirit of Saint Paul, greatest of apostles, the Catholic can confidently proclaim:

If God is for us, who is against us?

Who shall separate us from the love of Christ?

"If God is for us, who is against us?" Words of victory, words with the ring of triumph in every syllable! For Christ is always close beside him, if he but open his eyes to look and find Him—in Holy Communion, sacramentally within his very person, where, for the quarter hour, two hearts beat sturdily in place of a single faltering one; in the quiet church where a flickering red glow tells him that the Son of Mary is at home, to listen and to advise; in the person of his spiritual guide, within or outside of the confessional. He is there—the Victor King of Easter Sunday: "If God is for us, who is against us?"

Looking, then, upon life with the eyes of faith, trusting in the sure knowledge that the Son of God Himself is walking beside him, feeling the strong grasp of Christ's hand on his own, the Catholic walks along the way of life toward the goal that day by day comes closer. And along the way he encourages others, pointing out to them the Christ their weak eyes cannot discern.

In the Face of Death

"It is appointed to men once to die,
and after that, the judgment."

These are awesome words for every man: for the sinner, stripped of all the protection of creatures, doomed to face alone the Person he has so brutally maltreated throughout life; even for one who has tried to live loyal to Christ and His Mother, destined to stand alone—how soon he knows not—bereft of his very body, before the great and final high court.

Awed such a one should be, but not terrified. Not when a man has looked life squarely in the face, has been living as a preparation for dying, viewing life as a going from God and a return to God. Not when he has heard "I am the resurrection and the life, he who believes in Me, even if he die shall live and whoever lives and believes in Me shall never die." Not when he has so often repeated in the quiet of the Consecration "As often as you shall do these things you shall do them for a remembrance of Me," grateful words spoken by a Heart forgetful not even of a single cup of cold water. Not when he has so often entertained as personal guest and intimate friend Him who is to be his judge. Not when he has fashioned a lifetime of rosaries, whispering without ceasing to one who cannot fail to heed, "Holy Mary, Mother of God, pray for us sinners now and at the hour of our death. Amen." Not when his innermost heart echoes in firm belief the words of the Preface of the Mass for the Dead:

It is truly fitting and proper, right and for our welfare, that we should always and everywhere give thanks to You, holy Lord, almighty Father, eternal God, through Christ, our Lord. For in Him there has dawned for us the hope of a blessed resurrection, so that those who are saddened by the certainty of dying may be consoled by the promise of future immortality. For the life of Your faithful, O Lord, is changed, not ended, and when their earthly home dissolves, an everlasting mansion stands prepared for them in heaven.

And so with the angels and archangels, thrones and dominations, and all the warriors of heaven's array we chant to Your glory an endless hymn of praise, saying holy, holy, holy, Lord God of hosts, all the heaven and earth is filled with Your glory. Hosanna in the highest! Blessed is He who comes in the name of the Lord. Hosanna in the highest!

Prayer for a Happy Death

O Jesus, while adoring Your last breath, I pray You to receive mine. In the uncertainty whether I shall have the command of my senses when I shall depart out of this world, I offer You from this moment my agony and all the pains of my passing away. You are my Father and my Savior, and I give back my soul into Your hands. I desire that my last moment may be united to the moment of Your death and that the last beat of my heart may be an act of pure love of You, my Jesus.   Author unknown

Prayer to Mary for a Happy Death

O Mary, conceived without sin, pray for us who have recourse to you. O Refuge of Sinners, Mother of the dying, forsake us not at the hour of our death.

Obtain for us the grace of perfect sorrow, sincere contrition, the pardon and remission of our sins, a worthy receiving of the holy Viaticum and the comfort of the sacrament of extreme unction, in order that we may appear with greater security before the throne of the just but merciful judge, our God and our Redeemer. Amen. [500 days, R. 642]

Heaven, Our Home

Going home.
What a joy it is to return and see old friends,
to hear familiar voices again!
Heaven is the final return home,
the meeting with old friends who have gone before,
parents, brothers, sisters, loved ones.
But much more, it is the meeting with intimate friends
whom we have never seen face to face before,
Mary, our mother,
the whole Church Triumphant,
the greatest men and women of all ages;
the saints, the great in the truest sense of the word.
And beyond and above them all,
God Himself,
the brilliant, eternal Light of Heaven,
the reason for all happiness there,
the One who makes heaven, heaven.
He who sent us among His other creatures,
instructing us to look for Him in them,
now calls us back to Himself
to find as our reward the source of them all,
infinitely richer and eternally inexhaustible.

Heaven cannot be pictured in our imagination,
for we can imagine only what we can see—
the things of this earth.
Since heaven is so different, we sometimes wonder,
will we not feel out of place there,
a bit strange and uneasy?

We shall not feel out of place,
strange and uneasy,
for we are home:
home with God our Father and His Spirit,
home with Christ our Lord,
home with Mary our mother,
home with the saints, the cherished sons of God.
And we are happy:
eye has not seen
nor ear heard
nor has it entered into the heart of man
what things God has prepared
for those who love Him.

Like the men of the gospel parable
we count no sacrifice too great to purchase the field
in which lies the hidden treasure.

With Saint Paul
we reckon that the sufferings of the present time
are not worthy
to be compared with the glory to come
that will be revealed in us.

"For the rest, brethren,
be strengthened in the Lord
and in the might of his power.
Put on the armor of God,
that you may be able to stand
against the wiles of the devil. . . .
Stand, therefore,
having girded your loins with truth,
and having put on the breastplate of justice,
and having your feet shod
with the readiness of the gospel of peace,
in all things taking up the shield of faith, . . .
And take unto you the helmet of salvation
and the sword of the spirit,
that is, the word of God" (Ephesians 6:10-17).

ACKNOWLEDGMENTS

America Press, New York, for excerpts from "Miserentis-
simus Redemptor" (page 143) by Pope Pius XI
and from "On the Sacred Liturgy" (page 143) by
Pope Pius XII contained in *The Sacred Heart En-
cyclicals,* 1954.

Benziger Brothers, Inc., New York, for the prayers taken
from *The Raccolta,* 1952 edition.

Bruce Publishing Company, Milwaukee, for "Prayer of
the Angel of Fatima" (page 19) and "Fatima
Prayer for Sinners" (page 61) from *Our Lady of
Light,* 1947, by Chanoine C. Barthas and Gonzaga
da Fonseca, S.J.

Burns Oates & Washbourne Ltd., London, for "Prayer to
God the Father" (page 24), "Prayer to God the
Holy Spirit" (page 52), "Prayer to Saint Joseph"
(page 80), and "Prayer of Contrition" (page 133)
from *The School of Love,* 1923, by Archbishop
Alban Goodier, S.J.; and for an excerpt from *Devo-
tion to the Sacred Heart,* 1924, by Reverend
J. V. Bainvel, S.J.

Catholic Evidence Guild, New York, for the "Prayer to
Saint Paul" (page 205) by John E. McAniff.

Confraternity of Christian Doctrine, Washington, D.C.,
for the quotations from the New Testament which

were all taken from *The New Testament*, 1941, Confraternity edition.

Confraternity of the Precious Blood, Brooklyn, New York, for the quotations from the psalms which were all taken from *My Daily Psalm Book* arranged by Right Reverend Joseph B. Frey; and for "In Atonement for Daily Neglects" (page 119), "Jesus, Help Me!" (page 120), and "Prayer to the Heart of Jesus" (page 39) from the *Triple Novena Manual*, 1943, by Monsignor Joseph F. Stedman.

Coward-McCann, Inc., New York, for the "Prayer to the Divine Face" (page 182), "Prayer for Detachment" (page 182), "Prayer for Forgiveness" (page 180), "Prayer for Mercy" (page 180), "Prayer for God's Protection" (page 181), "Prayer for Love of God" (page 181), and "Prayer for Suffering" (page 181) from *Saints at Prayer* copyrighted 1942 by Raymond E. F. Larsson, editor.

Filas, Reverend Francis L., S.J., for the translation of an excerpt from "Quamquam Pluries" (page 79) by Pope Leo XIII contained in his *The Man Nearest to Christ*, 1944.

Franciscan Friars of the Atonement, Garrison, New York, for the "Prayer to Saint Peter, Prince of the Apostles" (page 83) and "Prayer to Saint Paul" (page 84) from a *Manual of Prayers for the Church Unity Octave*.

The Grail Movement, Grailville, Loveland, Ohio, for the "Prayer for Apostles" (page 204).

Liturgical Press, Collegeville, Minnesota, for the Easter prayer of Saint Gregory Nazianzen (page 171) and the Christmas prayer of Pope Leo XIII (page 166) from *A Short Breviary*, 1942.

E. M. Lohmann Company, Saint Paul, Minnesota, for "Baptism" (page 5), "Confirmation" (page 5), "Penance" (page 6), "Holy Eucharist" (page 6), "Extreme Unction" (page 7), "Matrimony" (page 7), "Prayer in Honor of Saint Ignatius Loyola" (page 90), "Oblation" (page 10), "Prayer from the

234

Mass of the North American Martyrs" (page 87), "Prayer in Honor of Saint Margaret Mary" (page 91), and the Passiontide prayer (page 170) from the *Saint Andrew Daily Missal* by Dom Gaspar Lefebvre, O.S.B.

Martin, Janet, for the translation of Claude de la Colombiere's "Prayer for Love of God" (page 39).

Martyrs' Shrine, Fort Sainte Marie, Canada, for the "Prayer to the Jesuit Martyr-Saints of North America" (page 206).

Mission Press, Techny, Illinois, for "Holy Orders" (page 7) and "Prayer for Priests' (page 208) from *Ordinations, 1947*.

The Month, London, for "Offering of Masses for the Dying" (page 96) from a *Manual of Prayers for Youth, 1935*, by the Reverend Fathers Morris, S.J., Rickaby, S.J., and Keating, S.J.

O'Flaherty, Reverend Vincent M., S.J., for "Consecration of Courtship" (page 220).

The Queen's Work, Saint Louis, Missouri, for "For Parents" (page 103), "For Those I Do Not Like or Have Harmed" (page 105), and "Prayer before Communion" (page 158) from *Christ Jesus Our King* by Reverend Daniel Lord, S.J.

The Russian Center, Fordham University, New York, for "The Cherubicon Prayer from the Byzantine Rite" (page 9) from *Byzantine Liturgy*.

The Servite Fathers, Chicago, for "An Act of Consecration to Our Sorrowful Mother" (page 68) from the *Novena in Honor of Our Sorrowful Mother, 1938*.

Sheed and Ward, New York, for the "Prayer of Petition" (page 179) from *Confessions of St. Augustine, 1943*, translated by F. J. Sheed.

Sisters of Providence, Saint Mary-of-the-Woods, Indiana, for the excerpt from "Mary-Likeness" (page 63).

INDEX